BOXING
IN BLACK
AND WHITE

PETER BACHO

HENRY HOLT AND COMPANY • NEW YORK

Henry Holt and Company, LLC
Publishers since 1866
115 West 18th Street
New York, New York 10011

Henry Holt is a registered
trademark of Henry Holt and Company, LLC

Published in Canada by Fitzhenry & Whiteside Ltd.,
195 Allstate Parkway, Markham, Ontario L3R 4T8.

Library of Congress Cataloging-in-Publication Data
Bacho, Peter.
Boxing in black and white / Peter Bacho.
p. cm.
Includes bibliographical references (pp. 118–19) and index.
Summary: Text and photographs present some of the notable
heavyweight boxing matches of the twentieth century, featuring such
fighters as Jack Dempsey, Joe Louis, and Muhammad Ali.
1. Boxing matches—History—Juvenile literature. 2. Boxing—
History—Juvenile literature. [1. Boxing—History. 2. Boxers
(Sports).] I. Title.
GV1121.B23 1999 796.83'09—dc21 99-14086

ISBN 0-8050-5779-X
First Edition—1999

Printed in the United States of America on acid-free paper. ∞

1 3 5 7 9 10 8 6 4 2

Contents

BOXING
IN BLACK
AND WHITE

▪ 1 ▪
BEFORE
MY TIME

Sammy Santos

Sammy Santos was a fighter; it was who he was and what he did. From 1923 to 1933, he fought very well as a lightweight, mostly in West Coast arenas. But Santos's story didn't start in America. He was born in 1902 in the Philippines, when the Philippines was just a poor American colony that, along with Puerto Rico and Guam, had been acquired by the United States after the Spanish-American War. In 1919, he couldn't find work, so, like many other Filipinos, he left home. His way out was paid by the U.S. Navy, where he still used his real name, Macario, and served as a mess boy aboard a ship bound for America. One day, a white junior officer called him a racist name. It was the officer's unlucky day; Macario knocked him down.

After the ship arrived in San Diego, Macario became an unofficial civilian. He just left the ship and went "absent without leave." At that time, California was the worst place for Filipinos to be. The state already had a long history of racism against earlier Asian immigrants, the Chinese and Japanese. Filipinos, the latest large group of immigrants from Asia, were quickly getting the same bad treatment. Most white Californians, and many other white Americans on the West Coast, thought Filipinos were inferior to them, and little more than "jungle savages."

For Filipinos, surviving in California was hard. The only jobs available to them were low-paying ones, such as planting and picking crops and dishwashing. To young Santos, who'd washed enough dishes in the navy, neither line of work was attractive. But he didn't have many skills other than his strong back and his determination. Soon he began to think about being a prizefighter because he liked to fight. He'd been in street fights and discovered he was pretty good with his hands, especially his right, which knocked men down and, usually, out. Santos felt it made sense to get paid for fighting; it was something he'd already done for free.

So he turned—as many desperate and tough young men before and since have done—to prizefighting. For Santos, who also changed his name to the more American-sounding "Sammy," the ring offered hope, an escape from desperation. Among Filipinos in America, Filipino fighters were heroes; only prizefighters escaped much of the routine racism of daily life. The ring was one place where a Filipino or an African American or a Mexican American would be judged on his merits. On the West Coast in particular, where most Filipinos settled, Filipino fighters—and there were hundreds in the 1920s and 1930s—had an intensely loyal following. Their fans would leave the fields or restaurant kitchens, and, jammed five or six to a car, they'd drive all day or night just to see a fight. For them, it was worth it to see Santos or, later, men such as middleweight champion Ceferino Garcia fight in Seattle, San Francisco, Sacramento, Stockton, or Los Angeles.

Santos had his first professional fight in 1923. He had trained just a few months in the gym and had skipped amateur fights altogether. It takes more time than that to hone the full bag of boxing skills. A well-schooled professional boxer often goes through years of training and several amateur bouts before his first paid fight. As an amateur, a young fighter can develop his habits and instincts at a slower pace. He can perfect his fighting style against less-dangerous opponents. Only if he succeeds in this preprofessional phase does the prize ring become the next sensible step.

Santos, though, couldn't wait. An amateur career was for patient young fighters. He had no time to waste. He was broke, and he knew he didn't want to wash dishes or cut asparagus. He knew he could fight. Now, he just wanted to get paid for it.

From 1923 to 1925, he boxed in California. Like all young professionals, he started out in low-paying, four-round preliminary bouts. What he lacked in polish, he made up for in power, especially from his straight right hand, which carried him to immediate success.

By his seventh fight, promoters began featuring him in main events, the big-money bouts. Promoters, though, weren't the only ones to pay attention. Sportswriters began calling him "Socking Sammy Santos"; they featured him in articles.

Even the navy, which still had Sammy listed as Macario, read the sports pages. According to Bobby Santos, Sammy's son, Sammy told him the shore patrol just showed up one day and took him back to San Diego where he served a short sentence for hitting the officer who had insulted him. Eventually he was discharged from the navy. Bobby doesn't know whether Sammy's discharge was honorable or dishonorable and says he never asked.

After getting out of the navy, Santos resumed his fighting career. He was a full-fledged main eventer, and at that level, he faced fighters who could block, slip, or dance away from his right-hand bombs. Some could counterpunch effectively—Santos's wide-open, wade-in style exposed him—but he was always willing to take punches in order to land his own, especially his right.

And for a bomber like Sammy, the eyes become his op-

Bobby Santos backs his opponent into the ropes.
Photo courtesy of Bob Santos

ponents' favorite target. A punch can blur vision or open a cut on an eyebrow. Dripping blood from such a cut can blind a fighter; too much blood, and a man becomes helpless. This will force a referee to stop the fight.

Although Santos continued to win, his eyes were taking a beating. (Indeed, old photos of Sammy just after a fight always showed bandages over his eyes.) First, vision in his left eye—with Santos's orthodox (left-hand lead) stance, his left eye was closest to his opponent—began to blur. The blurring was so bad that by 1926, Santos, at age twenty-four and just reaching his fighting peak, retired from the ring. He stayed out a year, restless, knowing that he could no longer do what he did best. Worse, outside of the ring he was just another undesirable Filipino in California, a proud, accomplished man expected to wash dishes, wait on tables, or pick crops.

In 1927 a telegram ended his retirement. Santos was offered five thousand dollars—a huge sum at the time—for a fight in Cleveland. Of course, there were risks. He was rusty, and the vision in his left eye was still blurred. Fighting would only make it worse.

Still, the choice was easy for Sammy Santos, a fighter by instinct and by trade. He took the fight and knocked out Ray Miller—a good fighter from Philadelphia, a legendary fight town—in the first round. His career was back on track.

Santos then returned to California, headlining cards there and later in Washington State. In Seattle in 1931, he fought Tod Morgan, a former junior lightweight champion. The fight was important for both men. Morgan had put on weight so that he could fight as a lightweight. He was hoping for a title shot in the heavier division. Santos had his own title hopes, which a win over Morgan would clearly boost. Morgan took the sixth-round decision, but the call was close and highly unpopular. Many thought the aggressive Santos had won easily.

The controversy over the fight made a quick rematch inevitable. In the second fight, Morgan was staggered by Santos. However, Morgan survived, and overall, he boxed smartly, stayed out of range, and piled up enough points to win again.

For Santos, the first Morgan fight was a turning point, the beginning of the end of his career. Both men knew each other's fighting style well. In the past, Morgan had been an aggressive fighter, and Santos had trained for a brutal, midring slugfest. He loved the thought of that kind of fight and was ready, even eager, to trade heavy blows. What he got, though, was a different Tod Morgan. This one danced and jabbed and used the whole ring. Morgan waited for Santos to charge forward, and either moved away or counterpunched crisply. According to the *Seattle Post-Intelligencer*, the heavier-handed Santos had hurt Morgan, and, in the final round, had him in trouble when he "crossed Morgan twice with effective right hands, and had Tod covering up on several occasions." The *Post-Intelligencer* added that Morgan "was badly marked from the Filipino's punches." Santos, however, had failed to knock Morgan out, and from the judges' viewpoint, Morgan had done just enough in the earlier rounds to gain the decision. In the rematch, Tod Morgan used the same long-distance tactics with the same result.

During the next several months, a pattern became clear when Santos fought in Northwest rings. Other opponents copied Morgan, jabbing and moving, content to fight safely, pile up points, and last the distance. Santos still scored his victories, but now his record was being balanced with more defeats. His career was going nowhere and his goal—a world championship fight—had become only a wish. Worse, his eyesight was quickly fading. By 1932, his left eye was completely blind and his right eye was also beginning to go. Still, with one blurred eye, he continued to fight, and even win. He retired in 1933 after knocking out Joey Kaufmann in Tacoma.

The years after his career ended became hard ones for Sammy Santos. For a while, he made money training fighters in Seattle—the city was a hot fight town at the time—but then, what was left of the vision in his right eye disappeared. He had become completely blind. Worse, Sammy's wife died of tuberculosis and left him with two young sons. The younger of the two, Bobby, recalls splitting time between his father's tiny room in a Seattle Chinatown hotel and living with relatives in order to attend school. "I'd live with my dad on weekends and take him around the community."

Arm in arm, father and son would stroll through China-town. Sammy made sure his boy stopped in at all of his favorite places, the pool halls, the bars, and the gambling joints that dotted the terrain of the old, rundown neighborhood. A lesson that young Bobby quickly learned was that being blind wasn't the same as being helpless. At a bar

Sammy Santos (left) poses with friends, other professional fighters, from the Filipino community.
Photo courtesy of Bob Santos

called Mikey's, Bobby recalls, Sammy heard a loud angry voice. Someone was picking on Felix, one of Sammy's old Filipino friends. The bully was a six-footer, a burly man who dwarfed poor frightened Felix. Sammy told his son to take him to the bully and to put "my [Sammy's] left hand on his right shoulder." Bobby did as told. What followed was a Santos straight right hand, and a one-punch knockout. "Bobby," the old man then said calmly, "we better go now."

Bobby Santos, age sixty-five, is now the Secretary Representative of the U.S. Department of Housing and Urban Development in Seattle. He has an important position, overseeing public-housing and urban-renewal projects in the Northwest and Alaska. What Bobby does in his job helps the poor get decent housing and is years away from his own humble Chinatown roots. But he remembers those roots—that's why he works in this job—and believes that the poor must be heard.

He remembers as well the respect everyone had for his father, a man who never backed down. He never saw his father fight, at least not in the ring. But when Sammy could still see and was training fighters, Bobby was being raised in boxing gyms. In those gyms, he quickly found out his dad was a legend. Bobby's sport of choice? Boxing, of course. "Being Sammy's son, it was expected," he says.

Bobby began by fighting his older brother in informal bouts after the professionals left the ring. They fought for money (dollars, dimes, and quarters) put up by the gym's regulars—the fighters, trainers, and onlookers. His early efforts weren't too successful. "He'd always whip me and make me cry," Bobby recalls. Still, he kept boxing, and by high school, he was winning amateur matches regularly. He kept fighting and winning through a Marine Corps tour of duty, then hung up his gloves. He'd thought about joining the professional ranks, but his father warned him not to. A prizefighter has to always be hungry, and Sammy knew his boy well enough. "Don't do it," he warned him, "unless you really think you can win any fight you get into."

Bobby, an American-born Marine Corps veteran, knew that while he had talent, he just didn't have Sammy's hunger to "win any fight." Sammy loved the ring in a way that was pure and fierce. In his case, prizefighting was a rare, perfect match of profession and man; the sport defined him. The loss of sight was a price he was willing to pay. Bobby recalls that his father never once complained, even after the start of total blindness. Sammy's love for the prize ring never changed. "If I was a young man today," he once said near the end of his life, "I would be a fighter."

Bobby didn't love the ring, at least not like his dad. He'd had a firsthand look at its cost. Besides, by the 1950s America was slowly beginning to open up. Racism against Filipinos wasn't as bad as it had been twenty years earlier. The son had been blessed by the timing and place of his birth. He had a range of better choices—education; a decent job; a home, not a hotel room, outside of Chinatown—that his father never had.

Bobby did get his education, land a good job, and buy a home, but in the 1960s, when the Civil Rights movement began to grab America's conscience, he returned to his roots and became an advocate. He fought for the rights of Seattle's poor. He joined alliances with other activists from across a broad ethnic spectrum. Together, they fought the bitter, sometimes dangerous, political fights—through community organizing, demonstrations, and building-construction shut-downs—that forced government and business to respond. In Seattle, major housing and health-care programs and an integrated workforce were among the many results of Bobby and his colleagues' hard work. Although Bobby didn't love boxing the way his dad did, his years with his father and his years in the sport made him a fighter. It couldn't have been any other way. After all, he was Sammy Santos's son.

When Bobby was away from Chinatown (at school, in the military, or with his own growing family), Sammy would often be with another old Filipino friend, an ex-fighter whose ring name was "Mission Bolo."

Unlike Santos, old Bolo wasn't very talented, and he had taken too much punishment. He could still see, but the head blows had made him punch-drunk. Somehow, Bolo came to believe he was part-owner of the famous Boeing airplane company, and started to act on that belief. Bobby recalls that Bolo would frequently call a taxi and tell the driver that Boeing would pick up his fare.

Sammy Santos often took care of Bolo and watched out for him. Their friendship lasted decades. When the two ex-fighters would travel together through Chinatown, with Bolo guiding, it was a perfect merger of strengths: Bolo's good eyesight and Santos's even temper and good sense. When Santos died in 1971, Bolo draped himself over the coffin. His mourning filled the small mortuary and touched all present. Bolo couldn't be consoled. A part of him had died.

·2·
THE RING
AND I

Sugar Ray Robinson versus Gene Fullmer, 1957

My earliest memories are from the 1950s. Many of those memories involve my father and me and different bachelor "uncles"—most not even related by blood—all gathered around the black-and-white television set in my family's small two-bedroom wooden house in Seattle. We'd be sitting in the living room and watching prizefights, which were televised on Friday nights. Not everyone had a television then. It was new and too expensive for men making their living as poorly paid migrant workers, moving from one field to another in the spring and fall, and sometimes to the Alaskan canneries in the summer. By the mid-1950s, my dad had stopped being a migrant worker and had taken a steady job. Dad was lucky. Steady work allowed him to buy a house, support a family, and afford a television.

So our little living room became a gathering point for televised fights and a temporary stop for an always changing crew of Filipino uncles, who'd drop by if they were in town and whose names I've mostly forgotten. What drew them together was the love of a sport. I didn't know then why Dad and his friends so loved the sport—boxing looked hard and mean. I just knew they did. Almost forty years later, I can see their faces full of joy or disappointment. I can hear their grunts and screams, their curses and cheers at the action shown on the screen. I grunted and screamed along with them; their heroes and favorites became mine. And for my dad and my uncles, their favorite fighter was Sugar Ray

Robinson, the great welterweight and middleweight champion, and maybe the greatest fighter, pound for pound, ever.

Robinson was great for a number of reasons. He was beautiful to watch; he'd just glide around the ring and make other, slower fighters look stupid as they tried to hit him. But he wasn't just pretty. He didn't depend on his ability to dance away and not get hit. When the fight was close, and he needed to win, he'd step forward like the toughest slugger. Toe-to-toe, Ray and his opponent would both throw hard, fast punches. Robinson's were usually harder, much faster, and more accurate; he'd hurt his opponent more than he was hurt, and he would often knock the other fighter out. That, said my dad and my uncles, showed he had heart. In an America where color counted and where just surviving was hard, these men knew about heart. Yes, Robinson, they said, had heart.

When Ray fought, our living room was always packed with fans. The kitchen table was full of food; the refrigerator was crammed with bottles of cold beer. One night, Robinson was fighting Gene Fullmer for the middleweight championship. Fullmer was a tough, brawling middleweight from Utah. To a man, the crowd in the house booed Fullmer. They knew he'd be trouble for Robinson. He was dirty, they said, as the pattern of the fight became clear. Robinson would dance around the ring and throw punches from a safe, long-range distance, and Fullmer—who was shorter and much slower, but also younger and stronger—would move forward and try to make the faster Robinson stop moving. Sometimes Fullmer was able to pin a tiring Robinson against the ropes and would bury his head or shoulder against Robinson's chest. From there, he'd throw short punches at Robinson's body and head. Sometimes, according to my uncles and father, the hated Fullmer would hold Robinson or hit him with an elbow or even head-butt him—all illegal

FULLMER		ROBINSON
29	AGE	40
160	WEIGHT	160
	HEIGHT	
5 ft. 8 in.		5 ft. 11 in.
	REACH	
69 in.		72½ in.
	CHEST NORMAL	
38 in.		36 in.
	CHEST EXPANDED	
41½ in.		38 in.
	WAIST	
31½ in.		29 in.
	THIGH	
23 in.		20 in.
	FIST	
12 in.		11½ in.
	NECK	
17 in		15 in.
	BICEPS	
15 in.		12 in.

Gene Fullmer and Sugar Ray Robinson:
the opponents at a glance.
Photo: AP/Wide World Photos

moves. Those men in front of the television were longtime
fans; they knew how to watch a fight. They understood the
moves that I didn't see. Me? I wasn't even ten and didn't
know the rules. But I do remember Fullmer pinning Robinson against the ropes again and again. At those times, it
looked more like a wrestling match than boxing. Fullmer
was pressed in so close, Robinson didn't have any room to
punch back or escape.

Recently, I looked up an old newspaper account of that
night; I wanted to check my memory against recorded de-
tails of the fight. As it turned out, I wasn't far off. The *New
York Times* called the battle, which took place in 1957, "a

rousing fight all the way." Fullmer's two-fisted attack was so savage that in the seventh round, his head and body shots "drove Robinson through the ropes out to the ring apron."

I remember that Fullmer didn't knock Robinson out. The fight went the full fifteen rounds, and the judges decided that Fullmer had hurt Robinson more than Robinson had hurt Fullmer. So Fullmer won the fight. When the decision was announced, my father and my uncles screamed and cursed as if they had also lost the fight.

I didn't curse, but I was really disappointed by the fight's outcome. I thought then that surely Gene Fullmer was a bad man. He really wasn't. In the years since that fight, I've read articles in different boxing magazines on Fullmer. As a human being, he was surely not a villain. Fullmer was just a tough, honest, hardworking man. He seemed like a very decent person, maybe even nice. On that night, though, when

**Fullmer used a lifetime of ring savvy to win a
fifteen-round decision.**
Photo by Herb Scharfman, International News Photos

he fought Robinson, he used every trick he could to beat
Ray. He crowded him and kept him against the ropes so he
could hurt him and slow him down. In other words, he did
what he had to do in order to win. Fullmer did what any
prizefighter would have done.

If Fullmer was such a decent fellow, why did we boo
him? As I look back, it's clear it really wasn't Fullmer's fault.
He was a white man; that's what stood out. I remember that
his skin was very pale, as though he'd never seen the sun in
Utah. And since the 1920s, when my father and uncles
began arriving in America, other white men had told them
they could only work certain low-paying jobs and could
only live in certain slum neighborhoods and that "their
kind" wasn't welcome here. On some occasions, white men
had attacked them and had tried to break them down.
"Don't expect much from this country," these other white
men told them.

So why did we cheer Ray? Making heroes of fighters such
as Robinson was nothing new to my dad and uncles. They'd
watched hundreds of Filipino fighters such as Sammy Santos and middleweight champion Ceferino Garcia box in
arenas up and down the West Coast. Boxing arenas were
one of the few places Filipinos could go and relax and escape a tough outside world. After watching so many fights,
men like my dad and uncles became devoted boxing fans.
No other sport moved them as much—not baseball, foot-
ball, or basketball. They didn't like team sports, but they did
love the one-on-one challenge of the ring; they enjoyed the
drama, the skill, even the violence. I know now that boxing
reminded them of their lives in America, except that their
struggles—to build families, to buy homes, to find decent
jobs—were harder and went much longer than ten or even
fifteen rounds.

Robinson was a favorite because Dad and my uncles enjoyed his skill and his heart. They knew that with his grace, power, and speed, they were watching someone very special. More than that, though, Ray Robinson was black. By the 1950s, the great wave of Filipino fighters had long since retired from the ring. And although Filipinos, a brown-skinned people, aren't black, in our neighborhoods in Seattle and other West Coast towns and cities, African Americans were our friends and neighbors, sometimes even family members through marriage. Black, the old men figured, was closer to brown than white. At that time, Filipinos understood—even I understood—what poverty and racism did to minority communities. Maybe Gene Fullmer never understood that, or maybe he did. We didn't know. We knew Ray Robinson did, and because he did, a black man became a Filipino hero.

By the time of the Robinson-Fullmer fight, my dad and uncles knew what to look for: the strategies of different fighters; the key turning points of different fights; the quick little fouls—such as thumbing an opponent's eye—that might escape a referee's attention but wouldn't escape theirs. Dad and my uncles were men I admired, and I wanted to be like them. They loved boxing, and I made up my mind to love it, too.

When I was a youngster, that love inspired me to go to different drugstores and supermarkets and buy all the boxing magazines I could afford. And if I didn't have the money, I just sat there and read any article on a promising fighter or a current champion that caught my eye, until the owner or a clerk chased me out of the store.

On Friday nights, or whenever a fight was televised, I'd be in front of the television set, sometimes with my dad and uncles, but often alone, just watching the matches. As I got older, I was better able to understand some of the different parts of boxing—why some punches work in some settings and don't work in others, why some fighters never seem to get hit even while standing directly in front of the opponent. Slowly, I came to understand that boxing is a lot more than just walking forward and throwing punches. Anyone can throw punches; I knew that from watching and being in school yard fights. But boxing at its best is different. I came to see boxing as an art—a hard, brutal one, but still an art. The art comes in hitting an opponent, and, as the opponent throws punches back, making him miss and miss again. At his best, that's what Sugar Ray Robinson did. I wondered if I could do it, too.

My dad and my uncles liked the idea. My mom didn't. My mom won, but she also knew that in our poor neighborhood, kids fought. She knew a lot of old-time Filipino boxers, friends of my dad, with their smashed noses, scarred eyes, and in Sammy Santos's case, complete blindness. She just didn't want me, her oldest boy, boxing. It was too mean, she said. But she also didn't want me getting beaten up. So she decided that any self-defense system short of boxing— the Asian styles that were beginning to get a foothold in America, i.e., judo, gung fu (kung fu), or karate—was fine with her. At fourteen, I chose judo first, but found that my tall, skinny body wasn't effective against shorter, stronger players who'd easily move under me, lift me up, and throw me all over the mat. All I got from judo was learning how to fall; it just wasn't my sport.

Gung fu was next, and here I was lucky. Gung fu is a Chinese hitting and kicking art, and there are many different systems. In most systems, the strikes are set in prearranged patterns, kind of like a dance. The legendary Bruce Lee established his first school in Seattle. Lee was one of a kind because unlike a lot of other martial artists—who were powerful but looked stiff, awkward, and slow—he didn't believe much in patterns and the traditional way of training. They weren't realistic in a street fight, he claimed. In the street, where anything goes, someone can throw a move that's completely un-expected. Lee's moves were explosive and natural, and just as instructors teach in modern-day kickboxing, he stressed full-contact training with headgear, mouthpieces, and gloves. That way, a student landing a punch or kick could see if the blow really stopped or hurt his opponent. Unlike other Asian martial artists, Lee wasn't interested in the beauty of a move; he was only interested in winning fights, on the street or in the ring.

The school wasn't advertised, but I'd heard about it through friends who were just starting in some form of martial arts. By 1967, Bruce had already left Seattle for a television and movie career, and the school was left under the supervision of Taky Kimura, his senior student. Through a high-school friend, I got to meet Taky—a very nice man—who invited me to join the school, which was then located in a basement in Chinatown. Without a second thought, I signed up, and, much to my mom's surprise, began to learn the basics of boxing. The man who actually ran the classes, Roy Hollingsworth, fought as an amateur in Britain and boxed professionally in Chicago.

Bruce really liked boxers because they threw hard punches, they endured pain, and they usually won street fights. Among his students in Seattle were many boxers, both amateur and professional. In my thirteen years at the school, I learned a lot about boxing from Roy. He'd have students lace up the gloves and box in a small makeshift ring. I did that a lot, but it's one thing to box people you know and who are friends—where you often find yourself holding back a punch; it's another to fight a stranger who's trying to hurt you or at least make you look bad. For that I had to go outside to other boxing venues.

My main base became the Wallingford Boys Club in Seattle, which had a small boxing ring. My trainer was Van

Peter Bacho (left) lands a shot.
Photo courtesy of Peter Bacho

Taylor, a former professional who fought mainly as a light heavyweight, although he'd occasionally go up in weight to fight in the more glamorous and better-paying heavyweight class, if the money was good enough. Most of the boxing was between members of the club, but sometimes Van would bring in an outside fighter or take us to another boxing club. At those times, the bouts were informal but very competitive and intense, and I found myself in some very hot action where punches were never pulled. In these informal bouts, or "smokers," I did pretty well and credit Van for that. He'd taught me that a well-rounded fighter had to be able to fight different styles. To help me keep shorter guys at a distance, he taught me to rely on the jab—the punch of the hand closest to the opponent—and to move around the ring. When I fought against taller opponents with longer arms, my tactics changed. I had to keep moving closer to a point where I could reach them with my own punches. Van wanted to see me crowd a taller man against the ropes—what Gene Fullmer did to Ray Robinson—and take away his room to punch and move. At the same time, I'd dig hard, short punches to the body, and then hit the head.

I did well enough for Van to ask me one day if I wanted to turn professional. He said he'd be my manager and trainer and that we could make some quick money. He still had enough connections with local promoters and could easily set up the bouts. All it would take was a phone call. I was flattered and, for a moment, maybe even tempted, but I told him no. I was almost twenty-nine, ancient for a beginning professional. I'd graduated from college; I'd even graduated from law school. Boxing, at this low level, had been challenging and fun. But prizefighting was several steps up, and I knew the cost. I wasn't that hungry or desperate; unlike my dad and my uncles, I was born in America, I was educated, I didn't have to work in the fields and canneries. I knew first-hand that boxing hurt, sometimes badly, and that the pain only got worse the higher you went.

That was almost twenty years ago, and since then, I've moved on to other careers (from attorney to journalist, teacher, writer), marriages, cities (San Francisco, Los Angeles, Sacramento), and friends.

Still, the sport haunted me so much that in my two other books—a novel, *CEBU*, and a collection of short stories, *Dark Blue Suit*—characters who were boxers play major roles. Maybe it's because this sport is what my dad and uncles loved, or maybe it's because it's what I grew to love and old habits are hard to break. There's also boxing's symbolic value, by which matches become more than just sporting events. That was true for my dad and uncles when they cheered Filipino fighters and, later, Sugar Ray Robinson.

The most famous symbol-laden fight in history was probably the Joe Louis–Max Schmeling rematch in 1938. In that bout, Louis, the great African-American heavyweight champion, fought Nazi Germany's Max Schmeling; Louis was hoping to avenge an earlier loss to Schmeling, the only one on his record. The world then was teetering on the brink of World War II, and Louis was viewed by his fellow Americans as representing America and democracy. Schmeling, on the other hand, stood for a hateful set of beliefs at the center of which was "Aryan (German and Northern European) supremacy." The rematch was so important, it seemed as if the entire world was watching the fight, or at least listening to it on the radio.

The Louis-Schmeling fight shows that boxing is a good way for any person, not just a boxing fan, to look at attitudes in our world and in America. Boxing fans tend to pick fighters less for their athletic talents and more for what these fans think the fighters represent, and nowhere is this more true than in the heavyweight division, boxing's most glamorous class. Thus, most of the stories chosen for this book focus on key heavyweight championship fights in this century; the stories combine both the action—the blows thrown, the tactics used—and the hopes of the fans that each fighter carries, whether he wants to or not. And, unfortunately, what the reader will see, more often than not, is an America too often divided by race and by class.

At the end of the book, I've added two little stories that, unlike the heavyweight-championship accounts, have no real import but are worth telling because they show boxing can hook someone for life. They're set in Seattle, which was, but no longer is, a great boxing town. Still, the subjects in these two stories hang on to the sport because, like me, they love it.

No one can doubt the sport's hard, brutal nature. A fighter's goal is to hurt his opponent and, ideally, to knock him out. This sport has cost fighters their eyesight and sometimes worse, i.e., their lives. Boxers have died in the ring, and not just poorly trained, out-of-shape men fighting four-, six-, or eight-round preliminary bouts. Men with the very best skills have also died fighting for championships and for glory, sometimes before national television audiences. Today, even some of the survivors—like legendary heavyweight champions Muhammad Ali and Floyd Patterson—suffer from terrible damage. So why write about boxing for young readers?

As I've gotten older, I've come to realize that in addition to the reasons for my love of the sport that I've already mentioned, there's something else I find valuable about it. Years ago there used to be something called a "fair fight," a one-to-one sort of challenge—whether in the ring or on the street—that even the tough, bad guys respected. As I look around today, the notion of the fair fight among young people, both male and female, is harder to find. The headlines are full of drive-by shootings to settle arguments, or reports of packs of young people jumping only one or two individuals. Today's streets and schools are more violent than in the past, but also, in many ways, the tough young men and women are much less brave. Today, disputes are too often settled by shots fired from long distance or from a speeding car. Where's the fair fight or courage in a drive-by shooting?

Boxing provides another way to face adulthood, one that applies to both boys and girls. (Recent amateur and professional cards have featured a growing number of women boxers, many of them as highly skilled as the males. Women fighters are no longer a novelty.) The sport requires fighters to train hard, to be disciplined, and to compete within a firm set of rules. When they step in the ring, they have to fight not just their opponents, who have a good chance of hurting them, but also their own rising fears that they will keep to themselves. Even in a three-round novice amateur bout, those fears are real and well founded. After the match, they must live with the results; of course, winning's much better, but boxers also learn to own up to their mistakes and accept defeat.

Boxing can teach young people confidence, courage, and grace—important qualities they may not get anywhere else. It's not an easy sport to do on any level, but if a boy or girl does it, he or she will learn to love it, and the lessons learned can stay a lifetime. Those are pretty good reasons to write this book.

■ 3 ■

SOME HEAVYWEIGHT

HIGHLIGHTS

Jack Johnson versus Jim Jeffries, 1910

The historic 1910 fight pitting Jack Johnson against Jim Jeffries in Reno, Nevada, actually came about because of a match fought two years earlier in a boxing ring thousands of miles away at Rushcutter's Bay near Sydney, Australia. There, Johnson—a tall (six feet one), superbly skilled boxer-puncher—faced Tommy Burns, the heavyweight champion of the world. Burns, who at five feet seven had mediocre skills and the height of a featherweight, had carefully avoided the dangerous Johnson since winning the crown in 1906. Burns's championship was due more to good timing than to his own skills. Just the year before, Jim Jeffries had retired as the undefeated heavyweight champion. Like so many great champions, Jeffries had destroyed or damaged a long line of good contenders.

Into this vacuum the lucky Burns, untouched by Jeffries's raw power, emerged. He claimed the crown in 1906 via a decision over Marvin Hart, the first heavyweight champion after Jeffries. As the new holder of the greatest individual title in sport, Tommy Burns quickly set out to make money from his status through a series of bouts with almost every fighter but Johnson. Given Johnson's skills, Burns could hardly be blamed for avoiding him. He wanted to hold on to the crown, which he couldn't do if he fought Johnson. Thus, he signed to fight easier opponents in the United States, then later, boxers in Europe and Australia. However, even overseas, Burns couldn't escape Johnson, who followed him and publicly mocked the champion's heart and skill. Finally, in Australia, money (a purse of thirty-five thousand dollars for Burns, a huge sum by the era's standards), Johnson's public insults, and growing public demand forced the match.

During the fight, Burns tried to move in, hoping he could get close enough to land his punches. To do that, he had to slip under Johnson's quick, stinging jab—the punch coming from the hand held closest to the opponent (in this case, Johnson's left)—and hard, straight right hand. A boxer slips a punch by moving his head to the side as the punch goes by. But even when Burns got close enough to throw a punch, Johnson's sharp reflexes and commanding height allowed him to lean back and away from Burns's short-armed attack.

When Johnson wasn't frustrating Burns, he was hurting him. Almost at will, he'd pump his long left jab into the face of the plodding Burns. The jab is the most important punch in boxing, and Johnson's was the best of that era. An accurate quick jab is usually thrown to the face and is often thrown in rapid succession (double or triple jabs). Although it's not a powerful punch, it disrupts the opponent and keeps him off balance and worried about defense. It's also used to set up more powerful punches like the cross (thrown in a straight line by the back hand; in Johnson's case, his right). With Johnson jabbing and hitting Burns at will, then parrying (blocking) or leaning away from Burns's harmless punches, the bout was less a fight than a stage for Johnson's skill. The famed novelist Jack London, covering the match for the *New York Herald*, described Burns as a "small and futile white man," and the ring action as "a monologue by one Johnson."

Like the great Muhammad Ali more than half a century later, Johnson was an average fighter's scariest dream—a tall, dazzling, unhittable boxer who could strike at any time.

Such a fighter is not only invincible but he raises the game from its plodding punch-for-punch roots and substitutes grace, skill, speed, and imagination for a less talented boxer's physical stamina and raw courage. Johnson and Ali made their slower opponents look foolish, made it seem as though they should never have even agreed to the fight.

On that day outside Sydney, poor Tommy Burns must have wished he were somewhere else. Ringside fans said that sometimes Johnson seemed to step back, just like an artist admiring his work—in this case, the "work" being Burns's puffy, cut, and bloody face. Johnson's mastery was so complete that during the bout he'd taunt Burns mercilessly; sometimes, he'd even chat casually with ringsiders.

Finally, the end came in the fourteenth round with Burns on the ropes, helpless from a potent Johnson right hand. Sydney police then swarmed the ring to stop the slaughter, and Johnson was officially awarded the decision.

The sporting public should have hailed this new exciting champion. It didn't. The problem was that the great Johnson was African American, the first one to hold boxing's most precious title. The absence of black champions was no mistake. Other talented black heavyweights were never given a chance to fight for their division's crown.

While black champions had been acceptable to the white public in the lower-weight classes, the heavyweight title was special. As historian Jeffrey Sammons notes, "The holder of the [heavyweight] title stood as a shining example of American strength and racial superiority." The heavyweight crown was indeed special and was supposed to belong only to white men, a view held by many whites, including John L. Sullivan, a legendary former heavyweight champion, who'd once declared he'd fight all contenders, except blacks.

Sullivan only said what most white Americans felt. Racism was officially part of this country's laws, which allowed states to segregate public facilities, such as schools, on the basis of race. Though attitudes varied from place to place and person to person, blacks were seen by many in the white majority as inferior. Black men were typically viewed as little better than animals; they were considered a sexual threat to white women and competitors to white men. In general, African Americans were tolerated, but only if they were quiet and knew "their place."

These were the times of Jack Johnson, a proud black man who enjoyed mocking white beliefs, including the custom that punished interracial sexual relations. This custom had become law in many states that banned racial intermarriage. On a less formal level, white mob violence, which included lynching, was routinely used against blacks, especially against "uppity" black males.

Johnson knew white racial attitudes all too well. He was born in Texas, a former slaveholding state. Still, he chose to socialize with white women, a fact that was often photographed and noted in newspapers. White popular hatred and fear of him grew. Worse, he clearly enjoyed offending whites' feelings on this sensitive matter. For outraged whites, something had to be done.

That "something" began with Jack London, the novelist, who'd covered the Burns fights. London published a newspaper appeal to Jim Jeffries, the great former heavyweight champion. The message to Jeffries, who was white, was racist and blunt. Jeffries "must emerge from his alfalfa farm and remove the smile from Johnson's face. Jeff, it's up to you."

London's message created a groundswell in the white sporting public for Jeffries to return to the ring. Public interest meant a rich payday for Jeffries and one more chance to receive public acclaim. It was easy for London to stoke public racism and to appeal to Jeffries's ego. London was a

Jack Johnson challenged racial attitudes by associating
with white women.
Photo: The Ring

writer, a master of the words that made up the challenge for someone else to bear. It was, however, another matter for Jeffries—by ring standards, an old fighter—to believe those words, and in the beginning, he didn't. At the start of London's silly campaign, Jeffries declared he wouldn't return to the ring to fight the dangerous, much younger Johnson.

Jeffries's five years of retirement is a boxing lifetime, and in that time, he'd ballooned to three hundred pounds. Even at his best, Jeffries was a powerful fighter but not a quick man. His age and weight had slowed him even more.

Still, the white public's demand that the fight take place, plus Jeffries's own ego, eventually overcame his good sense. Jeffries could still punch, and punch hard. But could any of those punches land on Johnson? That was the question, and the old champion decided they could. He agreed to the fight, which was held on a sweltering day in Reno, Nevada, on July 4, 1910.

At the opening bell, the thirty-five-year-old Jeffries plod-

Jack London urged Jim Jeffries to "emerge from his alfalfa farm and remove the smile from Johnson's face."
Photo: Boxing International

ded after his sleek, explosive opponent. Jeffries's punches were powerful but slow, which Johnson easily slipped (moving his head or body slightly away from the punch) or parried. Johnson would then counterpunch (a tactic that lures a punch, then strikes when the opponent's fist or fists are extended and out of defensive position). Johnson's counterpunch attack featured swift and dazzling multipunch combinations that eventually sapped Jeffries's legendary strength and heart. Like a human heavy bag, Jeffries's main role in this match would be to take punishment. The blows Johnson threw would have dropped lesser men.

From the first to the fifteenth round, the pattern seldom varied: Jeffries threw and missed, Johnson counterpunched and didn't. So dominant was Johnson that, just as in the Burns fight, he taunted his overmatched foe. He also chatted casually and often with ringsiders, especially with Jim Corbett, a white former heavyweight champion who was working Jeffries's corner. By the thirteenth round, the end was no longer in doubt.

John L. Sullivan, writing for the *New York Times*, described the action:

> Jeffries's arms seemed like lead and he could scarcely raise them, let alone hit Johnson. As the gong sounded, Jeff walked away slowly. He seemed all broken up and refused to be encouraged by his seconds. Johnson was jovial at all times.

Mercifully, in the fifteenth round, Johnson dropped a hurt, tired Jeffries, and although the ex-champ rose, he clearly had nothing left. The *New York Times* reported that Jeffries had "lost his sense of surroundings and that the faces at the ringside were a blur to him."

This knockdown was just the start. Before the round

**After the barrage of Johnson's attack, Jeffries had to admit:
"I was too old to come back."**
Photo: Brown Brothers

would end, two more knockdowns followed. After the third
knockdown, Jeffries, now completely helpless and unable to
rise, was saved from a knockout by one of his cornermen
who set one foot in the ring. This was an infraction, and the
referee—Tex Rickard, who also promoted the bout—spotted it and declared Johnson the winner.

After the fight, Jeffries admitted what he should have
known all along: "I was too old to come back."

Johnson should have been able to enjoy the postfight glow
of his greatest win. However, the time for celebration was
brief. Most of white America, never for Johnson to begin
with, now turned completely against him. Across America,
towns and cities, fearful of increasing racial tension, banned
any film showing the Johnson-Jeffries bout. Even Congress

jumped aboard the racist anti-Johnson train by passing a law preventing the interstate transport of fight films. Although this law didn't mention the new champion by name, its target was clear, Jack Johnson.

Jack Johnson was no saint. He was a flashy black man and his appetite for sex was legendary. He had many affairs, even while married, and most of these were with white women. His white lovers were shown off to an angry white public, and eventually the pressure of public rage channeled through the U.S. Department of Justice, brought him down. In 1913, the Justice Department successfully prosecuted Johnson for violating the Mann Act, a federal law that made it illegal to transport women across state lines for immoral purposes.

In this case, the government's star witness, Belle Schreiber, was a white prostitute and a former lover with whom Johnson had traveled. Johnson was bailed out of jail while his conviction was appealed. While free, he fled the United States for Europe, where he was to spend most of the next two years.

Unfortunately for Johnson, his spending habits outpaced his ability to make money. By 1914, Europeans had more important concerns, like the start of World War I, and Johnson was an exile in a region at war.

With no ready source of income, Johnson knew he had to return home to fight in a big money bout. America was still at peace, detached and isolated from the brutal trench warfare in Europe. Back home, a heavyweight championship match still mattered.

But there was still the Mann Act conviction, which ruled out a U.S. title defense. The problem was solved by Jack Curley, an American promoter. Curley chose Havana, Cuba, for the bout, a site close enough to U.S. shores to create American interest. Johnson's opponent would be Jess Willard, a tall, rawboned "white hope" from Kansas.

The fight itself was scheduled for a grueling forty-five rounds—a sharp contrast to today's twelve-round championship limit. The larger number of rounds was a residue of the sport's bare-knuckle, unregulated past when a prizefight could last for hours. As the sport began moving into the American mainstream, other factors, such as the safety of the fighters, began to be considered; a limit on the number of rounds was one of these.

The fight was held on April 15, 1915, a hot (100 degrees), cloudless afternoon. The day eerily resembled the Jeffries-Johnson setting five years earlier. In 1910, the relentless sun blessed the younger, better-trained Johnson. Five years later, that sun, as much as Willard, would become Johnson's enemy. The years since the Jeffries fight had seen Johnson fall out of shape. In Europe, he'd enjoyed a comfortable life, as befitted the world's most famous tourist. Boxing, other than an occasional easy match, had become the farthest thing from his mind. But still, he didn't worry. To him, Jess Willard was just another slow, untalented white fighter, like the scores of others he'd beaten with ease.

Jack Johnson was wrong. Willard had trained relentlessly. At his camp, he'd turned his sparring sessions into brutal little wars; he often hurt his sparring partners. If he was to have any chance at all, such an intense, violent focus was necessary because Willard was a one-dimensional fighter. He was big and slow, the sort of fighter Johnson would have toyed with in the past. But like Jeffries, he was also strong and very powerful; he could take a beating and still knock a man out, but only if the man was dumb enough to stand in front of him or too slow to get out of the way.

Despite his hard training, Jess Willard wasn't Jack Johnson. He didn't have the champion's quickness or his ability to throw pinpoint punches. What he did have was youth, great endurance, and an ability to take Johnson's best shots and still stay standing. These were the key ingredients around which Willard's handlers built their strategy, which was to force the older Johnson to throw punches and tire out. It was well known that Johnson didn't like to move toward an opponent. As he'd shown in the Burns and Jeffries fights, he liked to carefully back away, take his time, pick his spots, and counterpunch after an opponent's mistakes.

Johnson's style conserved energy; it relied on cunning and quick reflexes; it was a perfect style for an older, out-of-shape fighter. In contrast to Johnson's approach, moving forward and throwing punches is a high-energy, exhausting way to fight—one best suited to young fighters who haven't taken much damage. It's the sort of style that requires great stamina, which is built only by hard training—exactly what Johnson hadn't done. From the first to the twentieth rounds, Willard baited the trap perfectly. He mounted little offense, and simply absorbed punches. Johnson carried the fight; he found himself in the unaccustomed role of the aggressor— the fighter moving forward and throwing most of the punches.

Through the first twenty rounds, Johnson hit Willard often, and even cut him on the face, but he hadn't come close to knocking him out. Worse, the intense heat, Johnson's poor conditioning, and the high number of energy-sapping punches he'd thrown began to slow him down. Did the old champion have anything left?

In the twenty-first round, Willard, still fresh and sensing that Johnson was tiring, became more aggressive. The challenger began throwing more punches, while Johnson was quickly nearing total exhaustion. From that round on, Johnson threw few punches. The *New York Times* reported that in this part of the fight, "Johnson hardly struck a blow"; instead, the old champion focused mainly on "feinting at Willard," hoping to draw the stronger and younger man out of position. Johnson's efforts failed. Willard maintained his composure, kept moving toward his tiring opponent, and kept throwing hard punches that landed.

By the twenty-sixth round, the once quick, highly mobile Johnson could barely move. His superior boxing skills had evaporated under the sun. He was now too slow to get out of Willard's way. A hard Willard right to Johnson's jaw put the exhausted champion down and out.

Johnson later claimed that he threw the match to gain favor with American authorities and avoid jail. That is probably not true. If the fight were fixed, surely twenty-six rounds under a grueling sun would be too long for an aging, out-of-shape fighter to carry on such a painful show. Just as surely, Johnson did not benefit from his defeat. He eventually returned to the United States and served his time.

With his loss, Johnson faded as the main focus of white America's resentment, fear, and rage. A white man, Jess Willard, had taken the championship. Willard was followed by a parade of other white men. For white Americans, racial order had been restored. A white man was again holding the most important individual title in sport.

Still, Jack Johnson's significance cannot be denied because the history of American sports is also the history of America. Johnson's victories over Burns, and especially over Jeffries, declared that a black man, under fair conditions, could compete with and defeat a white man. Through his skilled fists, Jack Johnson taught this most valuable lesson, but it was one his country had yet to learn.

Gene Tunney versus Jack Dempsey, 1926 and 1927

American fight fans have always been fascinated with sluggers, the bigger the better. The reason is simple. A slugger, even when he's losing badly, is still a dangerous fighter. With a single lightning punch, he can change the course of a losing fight, and maybe even win it. Jack Dempsey landed just such a punch in his 1927 bout against Gene Tunney, a master boxer who'd taken Dempsey's heavyweight title the year before. In the first fight, the slick Tunney had used all of his skills—better movement, better jab, better defense—to confuse Dempsey and hit him at will. Through the first six rounds of their rematch, Tunney was on his way to doing the same thing. Then came the seventh, with Tunney backed against the ropes and Dempsey advancing. Dempsey threw a perfect left hook that landed flush on the champion's jaw. Tunney crumpled to the canvas, badly shaken, but he'd trained hard and was in superb fighting shape. The crowd was screaming. Could Tunney rise? Or would Dempsey's single powerful punch allow him to make history and reclaim the title, something no other ex-heavyweight champion had done up to that time?

Dempsey's seventh-round left hook produced most of the drama of the two Dempsey-Tunney fights and is still one of the most famous single punches in one of the most famous fights in heavyweight history. And maybe it's fitting that this punch is remembered because while Jack Dempsey is a boxing legend, no one really remembers Gene Tunney.

Jack Dempsey was known as a devastatingly brutal fighter.
Here George Bellows's painting captures the moment he
drove Argentine challenger Luis Firpo out of the ring.
George Bellows's Dempsey and Firpo, *collection of the*
Whitney Museum of American Art, New York

The truth is Tunney badly needed to fight Dempsey. He
needed Dempsey's relentless fighting style—a style fueled
by rage and a history of tough days in hobo camps—to balance his own thoughtful approach of jabbing, moving, and
counterpunching. For Dempsey, boxing was a very well-
paid and legal excuse to hurt another man badly, as he'd
hurt poor Jess Willard from whom he'd taken the crown
and, later, the Argentine challenger Luis Firpo, "the Wild
Bull of the Pampas." The Firpo-Dempsey bout was a wild
brawl. In the first round alone, both fighters abandoned defense; seven knockdowns were scored, five by Dempsey, the

eventual winner, who knocked out Firpo in the second round.

In contrast to Dempsey's bouts, most of Tunney's matches were tame. They had little of the drama or excitement of any fight involving Dempsey. Instead, a typical Tunney fight showcased his keen ring intelligence, his ability to turn a violent contest into a chess match. Tunney was content to let a fight go the distance and win by decision.

Tunney had to rely on his mind. At just over six feet one, he was slightly taller than Dempsey but not nearly as strong. In contrast to the muscular Dempsey, who weighed 190 pounds, Tunney, just five pounds lighter, seemed almost thin. And although his jab, the key punch of the cunning fighter, was quick, it lacked the velocity and power of an earlier thinking heavyweight, the great Jack Johnson. Finally, Tunney's foot speed, a trait especially important to effective defense, wasn't nearly as fast as that of a future legend, the elusive Muhammad Ali.

Still, Tunney had been successful and was a worthy challenger. That couldn't be doubted. Also not in doubt was the fact that the bland Tunney could never, on his own, capture the public's imagination. Tunney and Dempsey lived in the Roaring Twenties, America's fabled golden age of sports. Americans felt good about themselves and their country, which had emerged strong and relatively unharmed from the terrors of World War I. Americans were optimistic; they believed in an unlimited future and spent money freely. They invested. Some became millionaires.

Many Americans toasted the excesses and exploits of their sports heroes—larger-than-life figures such as the booze-swilling, woman-chasing, home run–hitting Babe Ruth and Jack Dempsey, who lived a fast-paced life, often in the company of gamblers, criminals, and other shadowy sorts. For

Dempsey, fighting had stopped being a priority. He took the
title from Willard in 1919, yet in the three years before his
1926 match with Tunney, he failed to defend his crown. This
was hardly the record of a fighting champion. Dempsey's advancing age (he was thirty-one in 1926) and a lack of tough
bouts, coupled with his love of luxury, dulled the edge
needed to keep winning championship fights. His predeces-
sor, Jack Johnson, had had to learn this hard lesson. Dempsey
would have to learn it, too.

On the eve of the first Tunney fight, Dempsey's best
rounds were behind him. Yet, the public still believed in his
fierce reputation. With three-to-one odds, Dempsey was the
betting favorite.

It wasn't just the fighters' boxing styles that clashed.
Dempsey was a poor boy who brawled his way out of poverty.
In comparison, Gene Tunney enjoyed a comfortable, secure
upbringing. He was born in the Greenwich Village neighborhood of New York City, then and now a center for literature and the arts. Tunney was also sober and read books, and,
unlike Dempsey, who'd avoided the military, he'd served in
the Marine Corps during World War I.

"The Fighting Marine," the press called Tunney, but unlike the swaggering marine image, Tunney was always
thoughtful and polite. Although *prim* seems an odd description for an ex-marine, topflight prizefighter, Gene Tunney
was prim, or near it anyway.

Unfortunately for Tunney, American fight fans have for-
ever been drawn to sluggers, from Dempsey to Rocky Marciano, and, more recently, to the great Panamanian Roberto
Duran (who held titles in four weight classes, and either
fought, or had televised, most of his biggest bouts in America) and former heavyweight champion Mike Tyson. While
boxers with more-rounded (both defensive and offensive)
skills—fighters such as the great former triple-crown holder

from Puerto Rico, Wilfredo Benitez (who beat Duran), or any number of fine, classic jab-first champions from Great Britain (lightweight Ken Buchanan, light heavyweight John Conteh, middleweight Alan Minter, etc.)—have flourished in other cultures, American fight fans have always loved savage, successful "bangers" like Dempsey. American fans often yawn at defense, seem to barely tolerate the jab, and hate fights that go the distance and have to be decided by judges. Of course, other, more stylish boxers—such as Ray Robinson, Ray Leonard, and, of course, Muhammad Ali—have also thrived in American rings, but they have had either overwhelming talent (Robinson) or a combination of talent and charisma that showed well on television (Leonard and Ali).

The dull but skillful Tunney was a promoter's nightmare in a nation hooked on excess and drama. It's Dempsey who's remembered; Gene Tunney was just an opponent the great champion fought. Dempsey was the magnet for the public's attention, if not affection; he had unmistakable charisma. His ferocity, his string of brutal bouts, and his controversial lifestyle—from avoiding the military to choosing his shady friends—fascinated not just fight fans, but Americans in general. Many of these fans would have cheered Abel, but would have paid to see Cain.

By the thousands, boxing fans flocked to Dempsey's matches, more than a few hoping he'd lose. But they came, and that was the important point. (Gate receipts at the two Dempsey-Tunney bouts were records for the time, $1,895.73 and $2,658.66, respectively.) The barrels of cash spent for tickets handsomely rewarded those tied to a Jack Dempsey fight—promoters, opponents, managers, trainers. The same couldn't be said of Gene Tunney, who fought with great skill but was outside of boxing's most lucrative limelight.

In a sense, Dempsey's appeal/repulsiveness to the public

is like that of modern heavyweight "outlaw" Mike Tyson—twice a champion, and a Dempsey admirer. For many, Tyson's public image—his outside-the-ring problems that included a prison sentence, and his brutal fighting style—were the main draws in his major bouts, including two losses to Evander Holyfield.

Like Tunney, Holyfield is an excellent boxer and warmly regarded as a sober, decent man. But just as the case was for Tunney with Dempsey, Holyfield's fearsome opponent was the draw in both Tyson-Holyfield bouts; some paid to see Tyson win, others paid to see him lose.

Tyson's grip on the public imagination can be shown by the following: The top four pay-per-view events of all time are Mike Tyson fights. The top two are his fights (1996 and 1997) with Holyfield, which isn't surprising because both were memorable bouts featuring great fighters. The fourth is a 1996 championship bout against a good fighter, Frank Bruno. However, in third place is Tyson's 1995 fight against Peter McNeely, who was average at best. What drew the public interest to this mismatch (McNeely lost in the first round) were the circumstances—this was Tyson's first fight after his release from prison for a rape conviction.

Boxing's popularity received a boost after Tyson bit Holyfield's ear in their second fight. In a 1997 article in *USA Today*, fight promoter Bob Arum stated that "Tyson and the despicable thing he did made boxing hot. . . . It's a commentary on the people, more than anything else." Arum's right; the public's reaction is a commentary, and a sad one, but it shouldn't be surprising. Boxing's hard-punching "bad boys" have always intrigued Americans. It's just as true now as it was in Jack Dempsey's day.

Although Dempsey never bit Tunney, he probably should have thought about it. In most of the rounds in both fights, Tunney boxed (not bit) Dempsey's ears off. Tunney's skilled left jab continuously kept Dempsey off balance and caused damage, while his movement and smart use of the entire ring made him hard to hit.

More important, he outfought Dempsey at just the right moments—for instance, after Dempsey had landed a hard blow. At such times in a boxer-slugger matchup, it's very important for a boxer to step out of character and give up caution; he has to move in and fire back hard in order to stop, or at least slow down, a slugger's building confidence and momentum. In both fights, Gene Tunney did this often. His flurries were accurate and hard and showed his army of doubters that he was more than just a light-punching, "safety-first," clever boxer with a deep defensive bag of tricks. The flurries also showed Dempsey that his aggressive, forward-moving style—so fearsome in the past and the only way he knew how to fight—would bring him his fair share of pain.

Tunney's complete mastery of Dempsey was evident as early as the first round of their first fight. In that round, he boxed Dempsey and used the ring smartly. Mostly, he stayed away from Dempsey and was hard to hit. But occasionally, he switched tactics and moved forward to throw hard punches. Near the end of the first round, Tunney became the aggressor and Dempsey, suddenly in trouble, was the one backed against the ropes. The *New York Times* wrote that "Tunney showered left and right swings to Dempsey's jaw and Dempsey was groggy." Between the first and second rounds, Dempsey "appeared very tired and his seconds worked hard over him."

For Dempsey, it wouldn't get any better. Tunney would dominate Dempsey over the next nine rounds, and although he never knocked him out, at the end Dempsey was a thoroughly beaten fighter. He was cut above the right eye and bleeding from the nose and mouth. In contrast, Tunney still looked fresh and comparatively unmarked. The judges' decision was unanimous in Tunney's favor.

The first six rounds of the rematch in Chicago were almost a replay of the first bout. As Tunney boxed smartly, Dempsey surged forward, taking Tunney's accurate combinations while hoping to land his heavier blows. For Dempsey, the pattern was a losing one, but part of a slugger's appeal is his one-punch ability, even when he's almost beaten, to steal a late-round win. (The most recent example of this phenomenon is George Foreman's dramatic late-round knockout of heavyweight champion Michael Moorer; until that point, the much younger Moorer had dominated Foreman.)

Then came the dramatic seventh round. The *Times* described Dempsey as "plunging in recklessly, charging bull-like, furiously and with utter contempt for the blows of the champion . . . suddenly lash[ing] a long, wicked left to the jaw with the power of old." Dempsey followed with a right to the jaw, then, suddenly, a wicked left hook thrown by one of the greatest punchers ever. That devastating hook landed on Tunney's jaw and snapped his head to the left, as far as it could turn. The champion, suddenly senseless, crumpled to the canvas.

Dempsey, ready to finish his prey, hovered over him, eager to club him again. This is against the rules. A boxer scoring a knockdown must go to the corner farthest from the fallen fighter. At first, Dempsey ignored referee Dave Barry's order to step back and go to the farthest corner to await Barry's ten count over the helpless Tunney. Barry correctly refused to begin the count until Dempsey obeyed his order, which he eventually did, but only after four precious seconds had passed. To this day, this is known as the "long count."

For most people, four seconds is not much time, but for the superbly trained Tunney, it was an important margin when added to the ten count. The extra seconds gave him

**When Dempsey refused to go to the neutral corner, he gave
Gene Tunney extra seconds to recover.**
Photo: AP/Wide World Photos

enough time to recover. He was up at nine and spent the
rest of the round clearing his head as he danced away from
immediate danger.

Tunney's full recovery was evident as early as the next
round, the eighth. Not only did he outbox Dempsey, he also
knocked him down on his way to a successful title defense.

After the rematch, Tunney fought one more time, a 1928
title defense in New York's Madison Square Garden. Tunney, the hometown hero, won, but boxing fans stayed home.
The bout's promoter, the famed Tex Rickard, admitted a loss
of $100,000, although, according to anonymous sources
cited in the *New York Times*, he was actually down $250,000.

Gene Tunney, boxing's skilled craftsman, retired after
this bout, as well he should. Even as heavyweight champion, he still needed Jack Dempsey, and not the reverse.

Joe Louis

In 1938, 124 seconds was all it took for heavyweight champion Joe Louis to finish Max Schmeling, his German challenger. But this was no ordinary first-round knockout, no out-of-the-blue single punch that lands just right. Those sorts of losses aren't too painful; one moment a boxer's conscious, the next he's not.

For Joe Louis, this knockout was entirely different—a complete, well-planned, first-round destruction of Schmeling, an excellent fighter who'd also once held the heavyweight crown. In those two-plus minutes, Louis must have hit him fifty times with his full arsenal of punches; many of those blows were heavy ones—left hooks and right crosses—and all seemed to land. In that round, Schmeling was down and up three times, then, finally, down and out from Louis's unstoppable attack.

For Louis, the win was especially sweet. In 1936, as the young Louis was rising up the ranks of contenders, Schmeling ambushed him. The result was a thorough beating capped by a twelfth-round knockout. The defeat, though, was just a temporary setback. The next year, Louis won the championship by knocking out reigning heavyweight king Jimmy Braddock. But even with the crown, the proud Louis knew he had unfinished business. He had to take care of Max Schmeling, the only man to beat him.

Almost half a century after his last professional fight, fans still talk about the second Louis-Schmeling fight. They also just talk about Joe Louis Barrow, better known as Joe Louis; he remains fixed in the American imagination. In today's era of multiple champions in each weight class, Louis was one of a kind. From 1937 to 1949, he was the undisputed heavyweight king, and the length of his unbroken reign—the longest in heavyweight history—helped make him unforgettable.

Louis's punches were powerful but accurately thrown pinpoint punches, starting with his thudding left jab that stunned opponents and set up his heavy-handed combinations. Each Louis punch was thrown with the right timing and just the right shift of the body into the blow. This sort of precise movement made him not just one of the greatest heavyweights, but also one of the greatest fighters of all time.

Despite the passing of so many years, old fight fans still talk about his ability to throw short, compact punches that would knock bigger men senseless. A short, quickly thrown blow is harder for the opponent to see or anticipate than a punch thrown from long distance, which makes it difficult to block or evade. Short, powerful punching enabled Louis, who, at a shade over six feet one and just under two hundred pounds (his best weight), was no giant, to consistently knock out much bigger men (Primo Carnera at 260 pounds, Buddy Baer at 250 pounds, Tony Galento at 225 pounds, and Max Baer at 210 pounds).

For Joe Louis, bigger, stronger fighters were no problem. His punching power was such that *The Ring* magazine, boxing's "bible," recently rated Louis as the best puncher of all time. The magazine selected him for the "proper and effective use of power resulting in [consistent] knockouts against quality opposition." Not many Louis fights went the distance.

Louis turned pro in 1934, just in time for the middle of the Great Depression, when desperate, unemployed Americans needed heroes. Louis became a hero by using his almost-superhuman talents. In 1934 and 1935, he had twenty-six fights and won them all, twenty-two by knockout. What makes this streak noteworthy was that the knockouts continued even as the level of competition improved. For example, Louis's last four bouts in 1935 included knockout wins over King Levinsky and Paulino Uzcudun, both leading contenders, as well as former heavyweight champs Primo Carnera and Max Baer.

Yet, it wasn't just Louis's fists that have made him an American legend. It was also his understated but confident and dignified manner outside the ring that swayed the public. This was especially important, since Louis was an African American.

The main roadblock in his career wasn't a flesh-and-blood boxer. Rather, it was the memories in the back of the white public's mind about the controversy surrounding Jack Johnson, the first and, before Louis, the only black man to hold the heavyweight crown. Other talented black heavyweights, such as Harry Wills who unsuccessfully chased Jack Dempsey, were denied a shot at the title. Louis's black brain trust—headed by John Roxborough and Julian Black, manager and comanager—decided early that this wouldn't happen to their fighter. They understood that for Louis to become champion, winning the white public's approval was key.

Roxborough was a wealthy realtor in Detroit, Louis's hometown, but his business, according to Louis, was just a front for his real trade—a big-time numbers (a form of illegal gambling) operation in the ghetto. Despite his criminal activities, Roxborough was well respected by many law-abiding black Detroiters, including Joe Louis. His wealth was proof enough of an intelligence and discipline strong enough to overcome white racism. Roxborough fully grasped the nature of that racism and the high barrier it posed to Louis's title hopes. He understood the symbolism of the heavyweight championship and the anger white Americans had felt when Jack Johnson held the title.

For Roxborough, the public Louis would become every parent's (including white parents) best, most successful (but still humble, God-fearing, and chaste) son. The image, of course, wasn't true, and as Louis became more successful, the gap between public hero and private man grew wider and deeper. Although married, Louis, by his own admission, was attracted to beautiful women, black and white. Some were famous, such as Lana Turner, the white film superstar, and the beautiful black actress and entertainer Lena Horne. Louis also admitted that in a fit of rage, he once struck Ms. Horne and came dangerously close to choking her to death.

Still, Roxborough's strategy worked to perfection; Louis's fists beat white opponents and notions of white superiority in the ring, while his public personality disarmed white hostility. Ironically, public support for Joe Louis grew even stronger after two matches, one of which was a loss: The first was the beating by Max Schmeling in 1936; the second was the eagerly anticipated rematch won by Louis two years later.

Before the first bout, Schmeling, a ten-to-one underdog, studied Louis carefully and saw a flaw in technique. Louis's lead hand, his left, was sometimes too low and out of good defensive position. This made him open to counterpunches to the head, especially a right cross (a straight punch thrown from the back hand of the boxer's normal "on guard" position). Interestingly, Jack Johnson, in a prefight article published in *The Ring*, spotted the same flaw.

A well-trained fighter holds his hands on guard, i.e., high enough to block oncoming punches to the head, while low enough to protect the ribs and belly with his forearms and elbows. Throwing punches takes the hands away from defense and opens the puncher up to counterpunches. To reduce this danger, a skilled fighter's punch will flash out and withdraw quickly to the on guard position.

The safest punch in boxing is the jab, thrown from the lead hand, usually the left. It is straight and fast and can be quickly returned for defense. In contrast, a hook—which is also usually thrown from the lead hand—is relatively risky because it opens up the fighter throwing the punch. Although risky, a good hook is also very powerful because it whips across the puncher's body and involves a full pivot of the body into the blow. (Trainers tell fighters to hook *through* the target, i.e., the opponent's head, ribs, jaw, etc.) If a well-thrown hook lands, it will hurt the opponent, and often knock him out.

To generate even more hooking power, a fighter may drop his elbow slightly so that when he pivots, the arc of the punch is reduced. This is the tightest possible link between the power of the pivot and the impact of the blow. If thrown this way, the fist becomes simply the striking surface of the twisting body behind it. In contrast, poorly trained fighters sometimes throw hooks with wide arcs that rely on muscles in the arm and shoulder. These "arm punches" are not especially powerful because the muscles on which they rely—the arm and shoulder—cannot generate as much power as a swiftly pivoting body.

In the first Schmeling fight, Louis's downfall started early, in the second round. Johnson and Schmeling were right. As Louis dropped his left to hook, Schmeling landed his counterpunch, a right cross on Louis's exposed chin. The punch was so hard, Louis admitted, he thought he'd swallowed his mouthpiece; he "was dazed, everything clouded over." Such a blow does two things: It lessens the confidence of the fighter who took the punch (Louis), and it makes the fighter who threw it (Schmeling) bolder. Confidence is very important, especially for an underdog. Schmeling decided to just keep throwing the right cross until Louis showed he could stop it.

That night, Louis couldn't. It was too late. His flaw hadn't been corrected during training, when a boxer is programmed to fight a certain way. He and his trainer focus on spotting weaknesses in his opponent, developing a fight strategy, and correcting the boxer's own weaknesses. In the middle of a hotly contested fight, it's too late to change habits. Louis's bad habit—his low left—hadn't been fixed in training; it wouldn't be fixed that night.

Schmeling kept throwing straight rights over Louis's left hand. One powerful right dropped Louis for a two count in the fourth round. Other rights staggered him in the later rounds. Finally, in the twelfth round, the *New York Times* wrote, Schmeling "punched and punched and punched with his right to Louis's head, to Louis's jaw, to Louis's face, and with each succeeding drive of his rival's fists Louis came closer to disaster." Finally, as Louis—"knees knocking, eyes blinking, head shaking from side to side"—reeled about the ring, a final Schmeling right to the jaw sent him down for a final time.

For Louis, the Schmeling loss was a painful but temporary setback, and fixing the flaw, his low left hand, was simple. He worked on it in training and tested it in the following bouts. When he returned to the ring, his power hadn't disappeared. Better still, his improved defense made him harder to hit with straight right hands. Louis won his next fifteen fights, fourteen of them by knockout, including a 1937 knockout of defending heavyweight champion James J. Braddock.

Still, even as the new heavyweight champion, Louis knew he had to fight Schmeling again to remove the shame of their first bout. The rematch was set for 1938. Between the first and second fights, the world had changed and was about to become much more dangerous.

By 1938, Germany was on the verge of war with its neighbors. The next year it would invade Poland and start World War II in Europe. Adolf Hitler was making claims of territory on neighboring Czechoslovakia. Hitler's National Socialist (Nazi) philosophy stressed the superiority of the Aryans, the control of the government over individual freedom (fascism), and the inferiority of non-Aryans. Hitler singled out German Jews to be the special targets of official government persecution. By the end of World War II in 1945, the Nazis would kill more than six million German and other European Jews.

After Schmeling's win over Louis, German propaganda touted him as living proof of the value of fascism and of Aryan supremacy. Joe Louis came to represent an opposite ideal, i.e., an African-American product of a free democratic society. That Louis should come to represent America's highest ideals was ironic because many African Americans and other minorities still suffered from widespread racism in the United States.

For Germans and Americans then, the 1938 fight was more than a boxing match. Despite the American public's growing hatred of Hitler, support for Louis and opposition to Schmeling were about as far as most Americans were willing to go. A majority of Americans did not favor going to war, even to stop Hitler. While most Americans didn't want war, they still wanted to embarrass Hitler and show up the stupidity of his doctrine of Aryan supremacy. The 1938 rematch was also a struggle of competing symbols—democracy versus fascism, and the ideal, however imperfect, of a free, multiracial society against government-sponsored racial hatred and persecution.

Almost all Americans understood the symbolic importance of this fight, starting with President Franklin Roosevelt, who met with Louis. Americans, Roosevelt said, "were depending on those [Louis's] muscles." Louis, of course, had his own personal motives for beating Schmeling, but he was moved as well by the deep hopes of his countrymen, black and white. Seldom has an American athlete carried such a unique and heavy burden, and seldom has an athlete succeeded so well.

For Joe Louis, the key to the rematch was to avoid the first fight's mistakes, one of which was underestimating Schmeling. He trained intensely and was completely focused on the task at hand. In the ring, his sparring partners imitated Schmeling and threw hard right hand after hard right hand. Louis had learned his lesson; he easily blocked or slipped the punches.

As training camp ended, Louis was confident, almost arrogant. On the day of the fight, Louis was asked how he felt. He said he was afraid he "might kill Schmeling tonight."

Just hours later in Madison Square Garden, Joe Louis almost did kill Max Schmeling. Mentally, he had set himself for no more than a three-round fight. He was going to go after Schmeling and wanted a quick knockout. He didn't want a decision. In his dressing room, he shadowboxed for half an hour, twenty minutes longer than his usual prefight routine. When he entered the ring, he wanted his muscles loose and in middle-round form. The early rounds are often slow-paced. A fighter uses them to size up an opponent; he will often fight from a safe distance and use his jab to probe for weaknesses. By the middle rounds, the pace will usually pick up. By then, the fighter knows the man in front of him. He must now focus on winning, and that's done by moving forward and exposing himself to danger. As he moves forward, he will throw heavier punches such as hooks and crosses.

That night Louis did not intend to fight from a distance or otherwise box carefully; he would stalk Schmeling and throw hard blows from the start. Joe Louis was the heavyweight champion, and especially in his bout against this man, the champion wanted an early KO.

That first round is one of the most famous rounds in heavyweight-championship history. Louis quickly went after Schmeling with his heaviest punches—two left hooks to the head and a straight right to the jaw. Schmeling fired back a right, but this time Louis easily blocked it. Schmeling then tried a left hook that missed. Those two punches, as Louis recalled, were the only ones Schmeling threw.

Louis attacked again with heavy punches—left hooks and right crosses—that landed and drove Schmeling, now dazed, to the ropes. Trapped against the ropes, Schmeling was helpless as Louis continued his assault. Desperate,

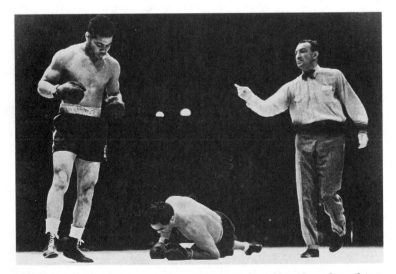

Joe Louis shows his mastery over Max Schmeling, knocking him out in the first round.
Photo: The Ring

Schmeling grabbed the top rope to keep from falling. Mercifully, the referee broke the fighters and sent Louis to a neutral corner. Schmeling got a one count before the referee signaled for the fight to resume.

Though still on his feet, Schmeling was through. He was no longer a threat to Louis, and only courage kept him upright. Louis quickly ripped into him with more powerful punches. Schmeling fell twice but got up both times. Finally, Louis finished him with two left hooks and a right to the jaw. Schmeling fell and was counted out after two minutes, four seconds of the first round. A ringside witness later told Louis that in that brief time, he figured Louis must have hit Schmeling about fifty times. The hard, accurate punches just kept coming and reminded the ringsider of a "pneumatic drill."

For black Americans, and for many white Americans as well, Louis's win was cause for celebration. In the long, difficult history of American race relations, the fact that whites cheered the victory of a black man was no small feat. In the 1930s, America was still divided by race; in other areas of public life—from schools in the South to whites-only major-league baseball—segregation was still the rule. Yet, the Louis-Schmeling fights, and especially the rematch, were hopeful and unique events in the history of American sports, and in the history of America as well.

For many white Americans, Joe Louis became a beloved public figure. Even Rocky Marciano, who was white and would later win the heavyweight championship, proclaimed his deep admiration for Louis. Ironically, the setting for that proclamation was the 1951 Louis-Marciano fight. The rising, hard-punching Marciano had just knocked out the fading, overweight Louis who'd unwisely come back out of retirement. Louis took the fight because he was broke and in deep debt.

After the knockout, Marciano went to see Louis in the loser's dressing room. Despite winning, he was so upset he was crying. Joe Louis was his hero, and Marciano's words said what many Americans felt about this man they'd come to love. "Joe," the teary-eyed future champion managed to say, "I'm sorry."

Muhammad Ali

It's really impossible to ask anyone who came of age in the 1960s what his or her favorite Ali moment was; there are just so many. Was it when Ali made fearsome heavyweight champion Sonny Liston quit on his stool, or, in the rematch, when Ali knocked him out? Was it when he unveiled his famous outrageous shuffle against Cleveland Williams and turned the brutal sport of boxing into something close to art? Or maybe it was the acts of raw courage—rising from a Joe Frazier knockdown in their first great match, or absorbing George Foreman's killer blows, or trading knockout bombs with the brave, noble Frazier in their third and final match, the greatest of all heavyweight bouts. Maybe it was all of these moments, or none of them; maybe it was the outside-the-ring memories, the silly Ali rhymes predicting a win, the ready laughter and quick wit, or his stances for racial justice and against the waste of a futile, controversial war.

Just as Joe Louis embodied the hopes of an earlier generation, Muhammad Ali represented the ideals of mine. He was young when I was, and Ali, as a fighter and a man, embodied my generation's restlessness, our style, our rebellion. Just as older fight fans passionately claim Louis was the best ever, we reply with equal passion that Louis, great though he was, would never have hit Ali. We also say that in the years since his retirement, we haven't seen any other heavyweight even come close to matching his power and talent. Finally, we swear, maybe against logic, that we never will.

Witty and likable, Cassius Clay embodied the spirit of his generation. His joining the Nation of Islam and changing his name to Muhammad Ali signaled a more radical turn in politics and race relations.
Photo by Flip Schulke

When Muhammad Ali, then Cassius Clay, first claimed he was the greatest, America should have listened more carefully. Ali would be that rarest of braggers. He was what he claimed to be—the greatest champion in heavyweight history.

It's been almost two decades since Ali's last fight (a 1981 decision loss to a much younger Trevor Berbick), and Ali can be measured against the handful of great heavyweights who came before him—Jack Johnson, Jack Dempsey, Gene Tunney, Joe Louis, Rocky Marciano—and those who followed—Joe Frazier, Larry Holmes, Mike Tyson, Evander Holyfield. Although these fighters were skilled, tough champions, not one was better than Ali at his best.

What made him so great? Nature, for one, blessed him unlike any other heavyweight. He was tall (six feet three), and, as he aged, his body filled out. Later in his career, a heavier Ali developed a potent right cross, a punch that wasn't as powerful when he was a younger, lighter man. His most useful assets, though, were his hand and foot speed, coupled with abnormally quick reflexes.

His left jab was blink-of-an-eye quick and always accurate. He'd see an opening, even the tiniest one—maybe a right hand guard slightly out of position, a half inch too low—and his jab was there. Because he was tall and had a long reach, he could throw the punch from a safe distance. Although Ali's jab wasn't powerful—like Joe Louis's—the jabs would come in flurries and tattoo the head and face of his opponent.

Ali, in one of his earliest, most famous boasts, claimed to "float like a butterfly, sting like a bee," and again, he was right. His left jab, the most dominating punch in heavyweight history, always set the tone for his fights. His jabs would sting opponents, upset their fight plans, and put them back on their heels—defensive and frustrated—hesitant to move forward. Opponents understood that in order to hit him, they had to first slip or block a punch that was much too quick. Still, when facing Ali, a fighter needed a plan, and the one that sometimes worked was to press him, to keep moving forward and get close enough so that when Ali's jab—or his less frequent right cross—was fully extended, you could counterpunch over or under the punch. At least that was the plan against Ali, and like many plans, it usually sounded better than it worked.

The most dramatic exception to failure in fighting Ali was Joe Frazier, a great champion in his own right. His signature punch—a powerful left hook—whipped under and over Ali's rear hand (his right) in their three great battles. In these fights, it was Frazier's feared left hook against Ali's quicker hands and greater mobility. Joe Frazier was an extraordinary man and fighter. To throw the wide-arcing hook well, a fighter has to get close to his foe. Against the taller Ali, this meant moving against a barrage of left jabs and quick straight rights. Yet Frazier's determination and discipline were such that if he couldn't block or slip Ali's punches, he'd simply take them in order to deliver his left hook.

In their three fights, Frazier's hook landed often to Ali's body and to the right side of Ali's head and jaw, frequently over Ali's right-hand guard. That guard was supposed to be held high enough to catch a counter left hook to the head, but Ali often held his hands low. At the start of his career, when he still had great foot speed, where he held his hands didn't matter. Opponents couldn't hit him anyway. However, as he got older, heavier, and much slower, his careless hand position would give the handful of tough fighters such as Frazier huge openings. The punches that landed would cost Ali dearly.

Most fighters, though, were not Joe Frazier, who'd fight—not box—from the opening bell until the end of the bout. In the last round of a fight against Ali, a typical opponent—assuming he lasted that long—would be frustrated and helpless, his face pulpy and cut from hundreds of jabs and other punches he couldn't avoid. Ali would usually be unmarked, saved from danger by his quick, dancing feet.

Ali didn't move like the average fighter who plods in, slowly stepping forward with his lead foot, while dragging the back one. Ali was no plodder. Instead, he was a jazz dancer who could spring forward or to either side, and could change direction without effort or thought. Like jazz, his moves seemed inspired more by the moment, and less by hours of practice and planning in the gym. This sort of movement dazzled opponents—no two-hundred-pound-plus fighter has ever moved so well—and added another weapon to Ali's already great arsenal.

He was so graceful and elusive, his opponents—such as the fearsome and powerful Sonny Liston, from whom Ali took the crown in 1964—looked slow and clumsy, even foolish. In that fight, Ali toyed with Liston and made him quit. (In the rematch, Ali took another approach—a first-round knockout of the former champion.) At the championship level, fighters are especially proud and skilled. But Ali's skills were so much greater, he would embarrass them in public by showing up their weaknesses. At least in his early years, he'd just hit them at will, then dance safely away. In that phase of Ali's career—from 1960, when he fought his first professional fight, to 1967, when he refused induction into the military and was stripped of his title—he could dominate a fight just with defense, i.e., by making an opponent miss badly as he danced away, to the back or from side to side.

**Defending champion Sonny Liston couldn't compete with
Ali's grace and skill.**
Photo: Boxing International

In the first years of his championship, he was the greatest
heavyweight who ever fought. Time flashes back to 1966 and
Ali's bout against the hard-punching Cleveland Williams,
who was nicknamed "the Big Cat." Williams was a strong,
talented fighter. He was so tough that when he fought Ali, he
did it with a bullet lodged in his body. Doctors couldn't

safely remove it, so it stayed inside him and he resumed fighting.

Ali was in his prime, and this match against the dangerous Williams was, for the champion, not much more than an exhibition. He knocked out Williams in three rounds, and he showed off the famous "Ali shuffle," in which his feet switched back and forth several times while he stayed in place. Like almost everything he did in the ring then, the shuffle was a blur. It was probably his supreme taunt, one intended to show his total control. For Ali watchers, the Williams fight was special; it was Ali at his peak, and the numbers bear it out. According to one account, "Ali landed more than one hundred punches, scored four knockdowns, and was hit a total of three times."

So superior was he in those years that he would also taunt an opponent by dropping his hands, then just lean away from an incoming punch. Of course, the punch would miss, but leaning away offended boxing "purists" because it broke certain ironclad rules. The first is that truly great champions move forward and throw punches. Dempsey, Louis, and Marciano followed this rule in their eras. Mike Tyson and Evander Holyfield follow it now.

Another rule is that a fighter moving forward defends against punches with blocks or slips. A good slip, done while moving forward, is very subtle. The fighter stays balanced and the punch misses by the smallest possible margin. Because he has not moved too much and has maintained his balance, the fighter is then in good position to effectively counterpunch over or under his opponent's extended hand.

Such rules are solid. They just didn't apply to Ali. His reflexes and foot speed were so quick, his body so flexible that his version of a slip was often to lean away from a punch with his hands down and at his sides, completely out of position. Often, he'd arch backward to create more distance.

Boxing purists said that at this point, Ali could be hit and hurt badly. But they were wrong; Ali was just creating a mirage. Again and again, Ali would suddenly snap forward and unleash blazing counterpunches at some poor plodding opponent who thought he had the great champion on the run.

Ali was like a bigger version of the late Bruce Lee, the famed martial artist. Each man had the natural talent and training to redefine his art, to break long-held rules and still succeed. Those who followed and thought they could do the same thing were wrong. Ali and Bruce Lee were each one of a kind. Jose Torres, a former light-heavyweight champion, once said that Ali's success caused other fighters to fail. Those fighters copied Ali's hands down, dancing style, and why not? Watching Ali on television or in person was addicting. He made the serious business of fighting seem so easy, so artistic and beautiful. But Ali imitators didn't have the talent to make it work. Rules, such as keeping your guard up, are for everyone else, for all other fighters—even very good ones—who aren't, and never will be, Muhammad Ali.

A smart fight trainer, if he had a promising young prospect, would do well to gather all of Ali's fight films, especially those from his unbeatable early years. A smart trainer would then burn them.

It isn't just for his boxing skills that Ali is remembered. He reached his physical peak in the 1960s, a time of national and world unrest and rebellion. In America, African Americans, led by Dr. Martin Luther King, Jr., were pressing for civil rights. Dr. King urged his followers to follow a path of nonviolence, even in the face of violence against them in the segregated South. King was an optimist. He believed in an integrated America, where color would no longer serve as a barrier to decent education, housing, and employment. He appealed to the better instincts buried in the conscience of white America.

Ali took the opposite approach. He challenged white America, even that part that was sympathetic to civil rights. In 1964, after beating Liston, Ali announced that he had joined the Nation of Islam, a controversial black religion that preaches racial separation and denounces whites as "devils." He then dropped Cassius Clay, which he called his "slave name," in favor of Muhammad Ali. Although Ali would later break with the Nation of Islam and its racial views, his conversion shocked many Americans, especially white Americans.

From that point on, each Ali fight become more than a boxing match. For many white Americans, Ali was like Jack Johnson, a black man who didn't "know his place." Many whites hoped Ali would lose, and, ironically, the best early hope for Ali haters was found in talented black boxers such as Floyd Patterson, a two-time heavyweight champion, and Ernie Terrell. Both insulted Ali by calling him "Clay," and both suffered as a result. Ali knocked out Patterson in 1965, and although Terrell lasted the full fifteen rounds in 1967, Ali's dominance was so complete it was painful to watch.

That same year, at the height of the Vietnam War, Ali was convicted in federal court for refusing induction into the U.S. Army. Ali said that war was against his religion; this argument was rejected by the district court, which sentenced him to five years in prison. Although he didn't actually serve the sentence—the U.S. Supreme Court reversed the decision in 1971—by taking this antiwar stance, Ali ran huge risks. There was every chance he would lose his title.

For Ali, entering the army would have been simpler and less costly. No one believed he would have been sent to the deadly jungles of Vietnam; a heavyweight champion was far too valuable to expose to enemy fire. Instead, like Joe Louis, who served in the army during World War II, he probably would have been given assignments to build up troop

Despite his superb physical condition, Ali was kept out of the ring
because of his refusal to serve during the Vietnam War.

Photo: David King Collection

morale and to strengthen support for the war. But the war was becoming more controversial as combat dragged on and more young Americans were killed.

Ali, whose statement "I ain't got no quarrel with them Vietcong" was one of the most famous single lines of the 1960s, also had a more thoughtful, important reason for refusing induction. "Unless you have a very good reason to kill," he said, "war is wrong." Just like Ali, many other Americans came to conclude that the United States had no cause to be in Vietnam.

By refusing induction, Ali joined two major youth-driven forces of the 1960s: an emerging sense of black pride, and growing opposition to the Vietnam War. In this troubled era, many young Americans of all races wanted major changes in society. They were challenging old attitudes that preserved segregation and institutions that backed a senseless war. For them, Muhammad Ali was a major hero.

Although Ali became a symbol of youthful rebellion, even among those who didn't follow boxing, his raised profile did not keep boxing authorities from stripping him of his title. From 1967 to part of 1970, when Ali was at his physical peak, he couldn't get a license to fight. Finally, a federal court ordered the influential New York State Athletic Commission to grant him a boxing license. The court found that the commission had issued or renewed hundreds of licenses to fighters who had committed crimes—including violent ones—that were far more serious than Ali's crime of refusing military induction.

During Ali's absence, the sporting public was robbed of the chance to see the best heavyweight who ever lived. In this void, less-talented men struggled against each other to replace him.

Jerry Quarry versus Joe Frazier

The 1969 heavyweight fight between Jerry Quarry and Joe Frazier was brutal and exciting. Quarry and Frazier, both hard-punching fighters, were viewed as the best of the young heavyweights. As they stepped into the ring, each had something to prove. With Ali gone, there was a lot at stake—for starters, a share of the crown once held by Ali. Both men knew there could be only one successor; the loser would return to the also-ran heavyweight pack.

At the opening bell, Quarry and Frazier moved to center ring, and, once within range of each other, began to throw heavy punches—left hooks and straight right hands. In the early going, they rocked each other; neither was particularly worried about defense or backing away. This fight was so raw, it seemed less about winning and more about making a statement of manhood in the ring. That meant no fancy defensive tricks, no dancing like Ali; this was fighting at its most basic—showing you could take the other man's best shot, then fire back with shots of your own to show you weren't hurt. By the fourth round, the tide had clearly started to turn. In this supreme test of wills, one will—weakened by the thud of heavier and more frequent punches to the head and jaw—began to bend. The referee stopped the fight after the seventh round.

For fight fans, the Frazier fight was Jerry Quarry's most memorable moment. Quarry was a heavyweight prizefighter; nothing more, nothing less. His confidence, his thick neck and broad, powerful shoulders gave him away. And, at age twenty-four, Quarry was a rare sight—a legitimate white contender in a sport and a division dominated by hard, hungry black men. Old-time observers marveled at Quarry's stunning skills. He had power in both hands and punched in tight, quick combinations that rocked foes, often draining their will and defeating them. His victims included Floyd Patterson, a former heavyweight champion, and Thad Spencer, who was then the number one–ranked contender.

Quarry loved to brawl, to just go forward and throw heavy punches, but his best skill was his ability to counterpunch effectively. By nature, counterpunchers are clever; they have trigger-quick reflexes and can anticipate an opponent's moves. They set traps, often faking exhaustion or pain just to lure the opponent into an aggressive, careless move.

A good counterpuncher lives for just that moment, when an opponent's jab is too slow, or the arc of his hook too wide. It is then, when the opponent has committed to the punch and has shifted his weight into it, that the counterpuncher strikes. His counterpunch, if perfectly timed, crashes into the face or body of his now-open target, the man leaning into the blow. The two colliding movements—a body or head leaning into an oncoming counterpunch—are misery for the person hit. Jerry Quarry was a master of this move. He may have been the best counterpuncher of all time in the heavyweight division.

On style and talent alone, Quarry commanded his share of attention from the boxing world. But it was his race that brought him added attention. Quarry was a white man in a black man's division, contending for boxing's most coveted individual title: heavyweight champion of the world. The late 1960s were hard times for race relations as African Americans struggled for equality. Major cities—New York, Detroit, Chicago, Los Angeles—were the scenes of political protests and race riots. In 1968 Richard Nixon was elected president, largely by appealing to the fears of working-class whites. The "silent majority," Nixon called them. For these people, Jerry Quarry was their champion, someone whose quick, powerful fists could symbolically restore racial and political order.

For his part, Quarry usually shunned the "white hope" tag. He said he wanted to be judged on his talents. Prize-fighting was already too hard, too brutal for him to also carry the hopes of white America. Still, it was clear the racial turmoil and increased black militancy bothered him. "The black man is being prejudiced against the white man by those who don't want equality but superiority," he told *Sports Illustrated*. "But everybody's afraid to sock it to the black man."

During these times, Quarry could never be just another talented fighter judged solely on his skills and record. He was white, even down to his proud ring name—"Irish Jerry Quarry." He couldn't escape his race. His fans wouldn't let him, and besides, it was part of his popular appeal, an appeal few black fighters could ever have. The focus on his race also made him rich and gave him chance after chance at big payday fights.

Within the heavyweight void created by Ali's departure were a host of talented, younger contenders ready to replace "the Greatest." In 1967–68, the WBA (World Boxing Association) held an eight-fighter heavyweight tournament, which eventually saw the crowning of Jimmy Ellis, Ali's sparring partner. Ellis was a clever but small heavyweight with solid, but not Ali-like, skills. His opponent in the championship bout was the once-beaten but heavily favored Jerry Quarry. Somehow, Quarry, on the verge of a title he could win, managed to fight one of the worst fights of his career. He lost the decision to Ellis after fifteen dull rounds and later claimed his poor performance was due to an injury suffered outside the ring.

Ellis was not fully accepted as Ali's successor. A second governing body for boxing—this one led by the New York State Athletic Commission—recognized the rugged Joe Frazier as its champion in the confusing post-Ali heavyweight era.

Boxing fans knew that a Quarry-Frazier matchup was inevitable; this was a match the public would pay to see. Both were young, powerful heavyweights struggling to make names for themselves. More important, one fighter was black, the other white. It was the perfect, moneymaking match for those racially hostile times.

Both men used styles that guaranteed fireworks. Both threw bombs, and few thought such a bout would go the distance.

The stocky, dogged Frazier was all power and heart. He'd win most slugfests just by shuffling forward to fire his deadly multiple left hooks to an opponent's kidney and head. No one ever had to look for Frazier; he was there, right in front, his forehead burrowed in the other man's chest. His record showed that because of his style, he could be hit, even hurt; the bullish Argentine, Oscar Bonavena, proved that by flooring Frazier. Somehow, however, he managed to rise and go forward, resume his attack, and win. What marked Joe Frazier most was his will—unbeatable—as he shuffled through a line of fighters often bigger and stronger than he.

Frazier was driven to prizefighting by memories of poverty. Like others before him and since, he saw the ring as a hard, honest road—maybe the only one—to a better life. The son of a South Carolina sharecropper, he came north with his family to Philadelphia, then and now a great fight town. There, young Joe took up boxing and honed his skills in that city's tough boxing gyms. He survived those early days and went on to an excellent amateur career, which included the heavyweight gold medal at the 1964 Tokyo Olympics. Still, a medal, even a gold one, couldn't pay the bills. He had to turn to the prize ring to do that.

Jerry Quarry had a similar story of hardship to tell. He was the son of Okies, poor dust-bowl migrants with long roots in the Southwest. In the 1930s, when an endless drought hit the region and destroyed small farms and towns, many packed up all they owned in rickety trucks and rusting old cars and drove west. Some settled in California, where better-off residents looked at them with suspicion and hostility. Jack, Jerry's father, drove his boys hard, as if their success would somehow erase his own memories of bitter poverty and shame. All the male Quarrys boxed; younger brother Mike also became a prizefighter skilled enough to fight for (but lose) the light-heavyweight championship.

Still, it was Jerry—the harder puncher, the heavyweight—who was the jewel of the fighting Quarry clan. Despite his talent and potential, he needed the championship to validate himself and his family name and history. Standing in his way was the champion, Joe Frazier, or "Smokin' Joe"—a nickname that didn't lie.

As the fight approached, the betting favored Frazier. He was unbeaten; Quarry wasn't. Plus, an early loss to a washed-up Eddie Machen, the loss to Ellis, and an uneven performance against a much older Floyd Patterson—which Quarry won, but not before fading badly in the last rounds—raised questions about Quarry's focus, his heart. There were no such questions about Frazier. Seldom had the ring seen a warrior so determined.

Yet, boxing isn't just a matter of courage. It's also about style and strategy, and that's why some oddsmakers and ring observers gave Quarry more than a good chance of snuffing out Smokin' Joe. They argued that Frazier's oncoming, left-hooking attack was perfect for Quarry's precise, loaded counterpunches. All Quarry had to do was be patient and exercise ring discipline. What he couldn't do was move to the center of the ring and just slug it out with Frazier. This type of fight was Frazier's game, one he'd win.

Quarry had to retreat and lure, then trap Frazier, who was relentless but predictable—shuffle forward, left hook; shuffle forward, left hook again. One of those hooks, the experts figured, was bound to be too wide or slow or both. At that point, Frazier would be open, and Quarry, who was quicker, could step inside the arc of the blow and beat him to the punch with hard, fast flurries. If Quarry played it safe and boxed, he could win.

The plan seemed flawless, but could Quarry carry it out? He had more than enough talent, but that wasn't all he needed. Did he also have a champion's discipline? Could he hold back his instinct to brawl, to prove his manhood by being tougher than Frazier and just taking and firing back hard shots? Just which Jerry Quarry would show up—the brawler or the counterpuncher who'd smartly outboxed the well-regarded Thad Spencer and almost everyone else? These were the big questions on the eve of the championship. Their answers would determine the winner.

For his part, Frazier knew what he had to do. The doubts that circled around Quarry never bothered Frazier. His fight plan was simple and proven. He'd just move forward and take, block, or slip Quarry's best shots, then left-hook him until he crumpled or surrendered. He'd done it to others and planned to do it to Quarry.

On June 23, 1969, the fight was held in Madison Square Garden. The capacity crowd—in fact, all the boxing world—was excited by this, the most significant heavyweight bout since Ali had won the crown in 1964. Ali's reign had been so dominant, the public had grown spoiled. Fans were almost bored by his string of victories. With this great heavyweight gone, the spotlight shifted to two talented youngsters—players in a drama featuring contrasts in style and race.

In the first few moments of the first round, Quarry moved to center ring and met Frazier. Quarry wanted to brawl. It was just what he shouldn't have done. For the first three rounds, they stayed put in center ring and simply exchanged power punches. This demonstration of courage and power was awesome, but it also sealed Quarry's fate.

Quicker in the early rounds, Jerry Quarry soon gave in to
Joe Frazier's relentless attack.
Photo: International Boxing

Quarry had some success. In the first round, the *New York Times* reported, Quarry's much quicker hands "slammed and slugged the champion with short left hooks and quick right hands that prevented Frazier from operating with his usual punching room." Quarry also rocked Frazier in the second round and forced him to step back, but not for long. Jerry Quarry had decided to fight a Joe Frazier type of fight, and in such a fight, Quarry was bound to lose. In the third round, a hard Frazier left hook opened a cut near Quarry's right eye. By the fourth round, Smokin' Joe had taken complete control. He just pounded Quarry with hard left-hand combinations. Quarry's response was to cover up as best he could and return increasingly weaker punches. By the fifth round,

Quarry's battered features are a marked contrast to
Frazier's postfight smile.
Photo: AP/WideWorld Photos

Quarry's battered face was covered with blood. After the seventh round, the referee stopped the slaughter.

Jerry Quarry had proven his manhood but had also lost the fight. He showed that despite his great talents, he didn't have a champion's discipline. Although he'd stay a contender and enjoy several more good paydays, he'd never fight for the championship again. (Quarry's brawling instincts shortened his life. In 1999, he died of brain damage from too many blows to his head. Jerry Quarry was fifty-three years old.)

Back in the locker room, Quarry almost seemed pleased by his performance. He felt he'd answered any questions about his heart. His show of courage was caught on film. Heart, Quarry had plenty of. What he still didn't have, though, was the championship belt.

The End of Exile—"The Greatest" Returns

When the courts finally allowed Ali to return to battle, he needed to work off the ring rust. He did this with two tune-up bout wins over good opponents—Jerry Quarry and, later, Oscar Bonavena. Joe Frazier was next.

The 1971 fight, the first of three Ali-Frazier bouts, was brutal. An older Ali was no longer the fleet dance master of his Sonny Liston–Cleveland Williams days. He was slower and heavier, less often on his toes and gliding around the ring. Even so, he was a great fighter.

His hands were still fast, and because he was heavier his punches carried more power. Flat-footed, he'd lean into punches that rocked Joe Frazier; Ali would hit him with powerful combinations as the shorter Frazier shuffled forward to land his left hook. Through the first fourteen rounds, the fight was grueling and close, with Frazier almost always the one moving forward, and Ali, the clever, accurate counterpuncher who retreated when he had to. Then came the last round, when Frazier won the fight by nailing a tired Ali with a hard left hook to the jaw. Ali went sprawling, and although he rose and beat the count, the win went to Frazier by close decision.

They fought again in 1974, but by then neither man was a champion. The year before, Joe Frazier had lost his crown to George Foreman, who was taller, younger, and more powerful than Frazier. During their fight, the muscular Foreman punched down at Frazier who, because of his

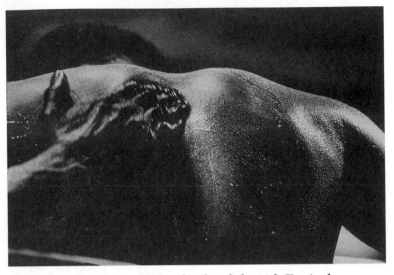

An older, slower Ali lost his first fight with Frazier by a close decision.
Photo: David King Collection

pressing style, was constantly in range of Foreman's club-bing blows. That fight was less a bout than a two-round mugging, in which Foreman dropped Frazier six times.

Because there was no championship at stake, the second Ali-Frazier fight lacked the prefight interest of the first. While the action in the ring was good—with Frazier press-ing and hooking and Ali counterpunching and moving—it just didn't match the drama of their first bout. Ali won an easy decision. But for much of the boxing world, his win had no real impact on the championship picture. It was just a fight between two talented but aging former champions. Only pride was at stake. It was widely assumed that the pow-erful Foreman, who looked unbeatable, would hold the crown for as long as he wanted.

As usual, Muhammad Ali proved the doubters wrong. In a stunning 1974 upset, Ali knocked out Foreman in one of the most famous heavyweight fights of all time, the so-called Rumble in the Jungle in Kinshasa, Zaire.

Against the stronger and younger Foreman, Ali fought only in spots to save his energy in the steamy, tropical African night. In the first round, Ali showcased his "rope-a-dope" strategy; he just lay with his back on the ropes and allowed Foreman to hit him. As Foreman waded in, Ali covered up (tucked in his chin and held his hands high with his elbows close to his body). Ali was very smart; he used the give of the ropes to help absorb the crippling power of Foreman's thudding blows. Ali's body was just a human target that the massive Foreman punched at will.

Ali's retreat to the ropes was once again against boxing wisdom, which held that if he was to have any chance at all, Ali had to jab, move, and use the entire ring against Foreman to wear him down. True to form, Ali showed that normal rules didn't apply to him. He hadn't told his trainer that he was going to fight Foreman this way. Ali's rope-a-dope tactic surprised his corner, who screamed at him, at least at the start, to get off the ropes.

But Ali's seeming insanity hid a brilliant plan that featured his strengths—exceptional courage and the ability to take a hard punch (undiscovered in his early days because he was rarely hit)—and hid his greatest weakness—his largely reduced foot speed. Rope-a-dope also exploited Foreman's many weaknesses—his crude, looping power punches which Ali often blocked, his inexperience in later rounds caused by so many quick knockouts, and even his massive physique which made him tire quickly. Rope-a-dope was a trap that Foreman walked into.

Throughout the early rounds, Foreman pounded Ali against the ropes. But the crafty Ali, by blocking his punches and leaning into the ropes to take away some of Foreman's power, stayed upright. In the fourth round, a still fresh Ali began taunting his tiring, frustrated foe. He mocked Foreman's inability to hurt a target that wasn't moving. In the sixth round, Ali, according to *The New York Times*, avoided the ropes and "moved more than he had been before in jabbing Foreman effectively and often." In the seventh, a badly tiring, very frustrated Foreman awkwardly chased the elusive Ali. His attempt, described in one account as "stumbling along," wasn't successful. By the eighth round, George Foreman was completely exhausted. He couldn't hurt anyone, much less the great Ali who then knocked him out and became only the second man in heavyweight history to win the championship twice.

Joe Frazier, though, was another matter. He was still a great puncher even in the later rounds and wouldn't make Foreman's mistakes. The Ali-Frazier series was tied at one apiece. They'd have to fight once more.

If Ali's sharp ring wisdom helped him to regain the crown against Foreman, sheer will was the key to the third Ali-Frazier fight. This 1975 bout in the Philippines, the "Thrilla in Manila," was probably the greatest fight in heavyweight history. It had been four years since Ali and Frazier's first fight, and over that time the rivalry had become intensely personal and bitter. Much of the fault was the verbally quicker Ali's. He was always baiting Joe Frazier, but his insults weren't just limited to Frazier's skill—a fair enough target—but also hit off-limit personal matters.

Frazier, according to Ali, was the "gorilla" doomed to "fall in Manila." The irony is that such an insult wasn't from a white racist. Instead, it came from the lighter-skinned Ali, an advocate of black pride, against the darker Frazier. Even Ali's most ardent fans winced. Frazier, a decent and honest man, didn't deserve that sort of abuse; such hateful words should never have been said. By 1975, it was too late for apologies. Joe Frazier, once Ali's conqueror, was, for Ali,

Personal rivalry brought Ali and Frazier together a third time.
Photo: David King Collection

still a lesser man and a stain on the great champion's record. To remove that stain, Ali would use all means.

Joe Frazier's response would have to come in the ring, but for the first four rounds, it seemed Frazier was over-matched here as well. Ali opened the fight flat-footed, the better to set himself and throw harder punches down at the shorter, forward-moving Frazier. Time and again, Ali's swift combinations found their mark, Frazier's bobbing and weaving face and head, but still the gallant Frazier pressed on. He had to. His strategy was no secret. The short and short-armed Frazier had to get close to Ali. He had to slip or block his jabs and crosses and then throw his left hook. Because Ali often held his right hand low and in poor defensive position, the right side of Ali's face and head was open to that hook.

Finally, in the fifth round, Frazier trapped Ali in a corner with no place to run. He then ripped Ali with effective body shots. Then came the sixth, a round in which Frazier landed two powerful left hooks to Ali's jaw. For the next several rounds, Frazier seemed to forget time, to forget the horrible beating by Foreman and the decision loss to Ali, as he steamed forward, slipped punches, and punished Ali's defensive mistakes with thundering left hooks. By the tenth round, the fight was even, and by the eleventh, Frazier had forged ahead. Ali just couldn't seem to stop Frazier's momentum. As the great sportswriter Red Smith wrote in describing this phase of the fight, "Frazier bludgeoned him remorselessly, pounding body and arms until the hands came down, hooking fiercely to the head as the protective shell chipped away." From the fifth to the eleventh rounds, Joe Frazier "just beat hell out of Ali."

Yet, somehow, Ali summoned enough strength and began to come back in the twelfth round. He speared Frazier with left jabs and right crosses. In the next round, a

Ali's many wins were not without cost.
Photo: David King Collection

straight right to the chin stunned Frazier, but Ali was by this time too tired to follow up on the opening. In the fourteenth round, the punches still flew from both men, but Ali's were more effective. He jabbed and crossed as Frazier tried to slip and counter with his left hook. Frazier's problem was that he was now almost spent. Worse, he was also nearly blind. Ali's punches had swollen Frazier's eyes to slits. In this brutal war, Muhammad Ali had just a little bit more. Eddie Futch, Frazier's manager, refused to let his man come out for the fifteenth round.

Ali had his precious win, but at what cost? Today, he suffers from Parkinson's syndrome, a condition brought on by brain-cell–destroying blows to the head. Among the symptoms are slurred speech and trembling hands. In the final Frazier fight alone—and Ali was to fight ten more times—he took 440 punches, many to his head.

In describing the Thrilla, Ali summed up its drama, power, and cost. His words formed an eerie description of the danger each fighter faces, one he had come to know too well after the last Frazier fight. "It was like death," Ali said. "Closest thing to dyin' that I know of."

▪4▪
BOXING
TODAY

Bobby Howard

I saw Bobby Howard fight near the end of his career. It was 1980 in the high-school gym in Sedro Wooley, a farming road-map dot just on the Washington side of the U.S.-Canadian border. I'd gone to watch Van Taylor, my old friend and coach, unwisely end his retirement and pick up some extra cash fighting in a preliminary bout. Van lost; his forty-year-old body just ran out of gas.

Both Bobby and Van were supporting players to the main draw, Pinklon Thomas, a future heavyweight champion. Then, Thomas was just getting his career started, and, as is always the case with potential champions, he was fattening his record on fighters handpicked to lose. His opponent, whose name I can't recall, was this handsome, soft-looking black man who knew his role. I had a chance to chat with the victim in the locker room before his fight/execution. I asked him who his opponent was. He looked at me sadly. "Pinklon, man," he whispered.

I then left the locker room for the packed gym just as Bobby's bout was getting under way. His opponent was "Rahway" Les Riggins, a hard-punching middleweight, who'd taken his nickname from the famous New Jersey prison where James Scott, an inmate and great light heavyweight, fought nationally televised bouts right there on the prison grounds. The fierce and fierce-looking Scott—who was bald, black, and muscular—usually destroyed fighters foolish or brave enough to come to Rahway.

Howard and Riggins were a study in contrasts: Bobby, pale and slender; Les, bald, black, and very muscular. I thought it would be a mismatch, but I was wrong. Bobby fooled me and probably everyone else that night. He used the ring, jabbed accurately and often, boxed smartly, and won the decision. I thought of that night in Sedro Wooley when I sat down to interview Bobby eighteen years later.

By his own admission, Bobby Howard was a juvenile delinquent, a self-described "dead-end kid." He and four other siblings were raised by a single mother in different Seattle housing projects. Life wasn't easy. Fighting in the streets became a way of life; it was what a skinny white kid living in a poor and desperate nonwhite world needed to do. Neither he nor Tommy, his older brother, would ever back down from a challenge. Winning street fights, though, doesn't count away from a dead-end street. His life was going nowhere, but a turning point came in 1971 in the form of Frank "Sarge" Little, a tall, old, and sour-looking black man.

As Bobby recalls, he and Tommy and their friends were on First Avenue, at that time a rough part of town. They were "hanging out, drinking beer" and making a lot of noise. Sarge, who was training fighters at the nearby Downtown Gym, got tired of the racket and came out to scold the group. He told them they had better things to do with their lives and offered to train them as a starting point. Bobby and Tommy decided to take Sarge up on his offer. After all, they'd fought for free in the street with bare fists. They figured fighting with gloves on and getting paid for it was an improvement. Bobby, who trained longer with Sarge than did his brother, credits the old man with teaching more than how to throw punches. He also taught him to be disciplined, both in the ring and out. One of Sarge's rules was for Bobby to get his education. "Sarge told me he wouldn't train me if

I dropped out of school," Bobby recalls. He wanted to box, so he stayed in school and, in the process, acquired the education necessary for a life beyond the ring.

After seven amateur fights, Bobby fought his professional debut in 1974 in Sacramento, California—a six-rounder—for $250. A year earlier, Tommy had turned pro and would go on to a successful nine-year, fifty-bout, mostly main-event career. In Sacramento, Bobby fought a draw, but he was hooked. He'd fight professionally for the next seven years, winning eighteen of twenty-six fights, but never hitting the big-money bouts and, along the way, paying the sport's painful price—a rebuilt nose, missing teeth.

Still, seventeen years after his last fight, Bobby Howard doesn't complain. "Boxing's like an addiction," he explains. "It just gets in the blood." He pauses, maybe thinking back to his own childhood. "A lot of fighters would be dead if it weren't for boxing," he says.

That's why when he retired from the ring, he didn't retire from boxing. Today, he's helping other kids, some of them dead-end ones as he once was. He trains fighters, mostly young amateurs, in the Seattle area. "I like impacting kids' lives," he says.

He does this by passing on what the hard sport of boxing and old Sarge had taught him: boxing basics and, more important, the discipline needed to do them well. "I dissect each move for the kids," he says. "I don't want to see anyone get hurt."

Working as a trainer isn't his full-time job; Bobby rushes to the gym only after a full day's work. The added hours in the gym sometimes strain his family life—he's married; he and his wife have a young daughter. Still, he says, his wife understands. Boxing, she knows, is in his blood; it's the part of him that gave him a chance, something he wants badly to pass on.

Coach Bobby Howard offers young people the same means he
found for a better life: boxing—and hard work.
Photo courtesy of Bobby Howard

In time, the former dead-end kid went over to the other
side and passed the hard group of tests to become a deputy
sheriff for Snohomish County. He is now a fifteen-year veteran. Sarge was right; staying in school was important. Becoming a cop brought Bobby security—decent, steady pay

and benefits and an eventual and inevitable good-bye to his
fighting career.

Bobby found that when he talks as a cop to at-risk kids,
they often don't listen. They see the uniform, hate the au-
thority, and block out Deputy Howard's warnings and advice. "But as a boxing coach, these same kids listen," he says.
Just recently Bobby Howard, the coach, "stopped two gang
problems in the gym." In a sense, it isn't surprising that in
this role, Coach Howard can reach these youngsters. He understands their anger and hurt, their problems, and the need
for boys or young men to face challenges alone and overcome them. In turn, they admire him: He came from
poverty to travel the demanding ring road and survived its
dangers; away from boxing, he's managed to build a life
that's decent and good.

On a cold January night, Bobby is working with two young
amateurs. One of them is a tall and rangy young man, Dimitri Sandeman. He weighs more than 160 pounds, but wants
to fight at a lower weight, 156 pounds. At 156, his six-foot
height and long reach would allow him to jab shorter-armed,
stockier opponents from a safe distance and dictate the flow of
the fight. He's a twenty-year-old junior college student who's
been in and out of boxing gyms since he was thirteen. When
he was younger, he fought in amateur smokers—unofficial
bouts, but often very competitive and good boxing experience. In three weeks, he will have his official novice-class
debut in a fight sanctioned by United States Amateur Boxing,
Inc., the sport's governing body.

Although it's a bitterly cold night, inside the gym, the
body heat from the fighters steams the windows. Bobby tells
Dimitri and Mark, another young boxer, to get ready to spar.
"Get sixteens," the coach says, referring to the large sparring
gloves, oversized pillows compared to the ten-ounce gloves

worn in amateur fights, and even smaller eights worn by professionals. Mark, Bobby adds, has been in the gym for about a year. "He just works real hard," he says.

The boxers patiently wait their turns as Bobby and one of the gym visitors lace up their gloves and help them with the rest of their equipment—mouthpieces, thick headgear, and leather protective cups worn on the outside of their sweats.

The young men then go to opposite corners and wait for the signal—a bell that rings every three minutes—to sound. At the *ding,* they meet in center ring. Immediately, the difference in experience shows. Dimitri is smooth and fluid; he looks comfortable as he bobs and weaves and parries jabs and crisp crosses. Despite his height, his upper body is loose enough to get under many of the punches. It's a good sign, and in this round it's clear he's taking his time, honing his defensive skills.

In the second round, Dimitri shifts to offense, and opens up with jabs and crosses of his own. His left jabs—usually thrown as doubles—land often and set up his other punches, his right cross and left hook. By midround, Dimitri begins hooking to the head more often, and some punches hit their target over Mark's right hand, which has begun to drop out of good defensive position. But these hooks are more like slaps from long range because they're thrown off balance. At the end of the round, Bobby talks to Dimitri. He explains what Dimitri already knows, that he must be balanced as he moves in if he's to hook with power. The young boxer nods; he understands.

Before the third and final round begins, Bobby imposes a condition. He wants Dimitri to work just on his left hand—good, stiff jabs and hard, tight hooks. "Forget the right," Bobby tells Dimitri. "I want to see some magic with that left." The less experienced Mark can box with both hands.

In this round, Mark again presses forward. Dimitri, limited to his left, jabs effectively to the head, then tries to hook off the jab. The footwork for the hook is still not there; his legs—which, ideally, should be apart, balanced, and coiled—are too close together. The hook slaps and doesn't jolt. Understanding a move is different from doing it. Still, Dimitri has time—three weeks until his debut fight—to fix the flaw.

After the spar, Dimitri towels off, then talks about his ring hopes. He naturally wants to win this upcoming bout, then later, the novice division (ten fights or less) of the local Golden Gloves tournament. He'd once thought that if he won the novice tournament, he'd quit boxing. It would be a fitting end to something he's "been doing so long." But now, he's not so sure. Why continue? According to Bobby, Dimitri's not a typical fighter. He's a white kid from Seattle's comfortable northern suburbs in a sport long dominated by the people of color and the poor; he's thoughtful and well spoken. Today, he's in college, and if he continues with school a four-year degree will open doors to a good life.

Given that, why spend the hours away from his books and assignments? Why run the miles in the cold January drizzle that never seems to stop? Why take the lumps that are part of this hard, sometimes brutal sport? Dimitri pauses and searches for the words.

"It's winning, especially in boxing," Dimitri finally says. "It's the most addictive sport." Bobby, the old dead-end kid, doesn't hear this, but no matter. It's a feeling he'd understand.

Jim Gilmore

Boxing isn't just multimillion-dollar bouts between famous champions determined to hold on to their crowns, and contenders equally determined to take them away. The sport's also about a lot of unknown others — referees, judges, sparring partners, trainers, and ordinary fans, without whom the game couldn't exist.

In his thirty-seven years, Jim Gilmore has played most of these roles. As a young boy, he trained at the Eagles Gym in downtown Seattle, which was once the center of professional and amateur boxing in the Northwest. The gym's now gone, a victim of the ongoing building and growth in this booming city. In a way, the old gym's passing symbolizes the state of boxing in Seattle, where the sport is dead, or nearly dead, but not many seem to notice or even care.

But Jim Gilmore does. By day, he operates a small neighborhood grocery store, which he owns. Running this store is a fourteen-hour job, seven days a week. And although Gilmore would prefer an easier line of work, what he has is convenient. The store pays the costs of a small boxing gym next door. Almost every evening, if he can get someone to watch the store, he can be found coaching boxing fundamentals — jab, cross, footwork, slip and parry — to a changing cast of boxers, or want-to-be boxers, eager to polish existing skills or learn new ones.

This gym isn't like the famed boxing gyms of Philadelphia, where sparring matches between talented and hungry men routinely become unofficial brawls of manhood and pride, and where Joe Frazier, like so many Philly fighters, honed his left hook. Nor is it like the Kronk Gym in Detroit, where the great trainer Emanuel Steward turns up the thermostat so his world-class fighters sweat more, work harder. Such gyms produce at the very least main-event prizefighters, and often world champions.

Gilmore would love to do the same thing, but he's realistic. Seattle is a comfortable town, made so by a long-running healthy economy that makes computer programs and commercial jets for buyers who only want more. Seattle isn't Detroit or Philadelphia, where loyal fight fans cheer homegrown boxers who are poor, hungry, and determined. Seattleites go to baseball or basketball games; they go to the theater and opera. They don't go to prizefights.

And at least on this night, it's pretty clear that those gathered in the gym—a group of about twenty males and females of all ages, shapes, and abilities—don't go to prizefights either. It's unlikely, among those gathered tonight, that anyone will ever fight competitively; some may never even fire a punch in anger, either in the ring or on the street. Yet, all seem pleased by the fast-paced workout and the sense that they are learning something that might come in handy, like the right form for the jab (snapped straight out, brought straight back).

As they go through their paces—hitting both the heavy and the speed bags with different levels of power, speed, and coordination—Gilmore, a lean, compact man, is constantly moving, observing, correcting, demonstrating. His own moves are crisp and precise—the moves of a good athlete, in his case, an ex-amateur boxer. His punches still snap and come in quick flurries.

"Get the hand back," he scolds a young woman who's just thrown a slow, lazy left jab. It had dangled for much too long and made her entire left side, from head to belly, open for a counterpunch. "Snap it," he scolds, as her next jab shoots out and back more briskly.

Gilmore's little gym isn't Kronk, but so what? He loves what he's doing, and besides, it's a way to stay in "the game," one he's loved since he was twelve, when he was first shown the basics by a local coach. Later, as a teenager, he'd learned enough to begin training at the Eagles Gym. There, older fighters—the professionals—would often pound young amateurs. Youngsters such as Gilmore were frequently used as heavy bags during sparring sessions, but they were better than the bags because not only couldn't they hurt an experienced professional, they could also move around the ring and give the pro good "target practice"; a professional could fire fast and hard combinations and see which ones worked. "The pros would tee off on you," Gilmore says.

Not surprisingly, many young boxers became discouraged and would never return after such a beating. Gilmore returned. "When I started out at Eagles, I got worked over real good," he says of those early days. He pauses. "But the next day I was there when the gym opened."

Why put up with the embarrassment and pain? he's asked. "I loved it," he replies. "I wanted to prove I belonged."

Eventually, his skills got better and he began to hold his own against the more experienced professionals. At one point, he even thought of turning pro. That sort of determination taught him lessons beyond the ring.

Gilmore was attending public schools that drew students from the city's rougher neighborhoods. As a youngster, he found that boxing gave him respect. He wasn't especially big or tall, but his hands were fast, and he'd throw them when cornered. Fellow students, no matter how tough, soon learned to leave him alone. "It was because I punched back," he recalls.

Boxing's discipline also helped him in his most desperate moment. At seventeen, he suffered a depressed skull fracture in a head-on automobile accident. He was in critical condition, lucky just to be alive. During surgery, the doctors put a polyurethane plate in his skull just above his right ear.

"It's about an inch long, shaped like a bean with a hump in the middle," he says, and smiles. "Got a photo at home. Want to see it?" The offer is declined.

The scar from the operation is now just a short, thin line, but it can still be seen. And even today, his head will sometimes throb. On some days, the throbbing gets so bad, he can barely move. Usually, though, he can make it go away by massaging his temples. The pain and the scar are permanent reminders of how close he came to dying.

For Jim Gilmore, the long road back ran through the ring. He thought of how much he missed boxing. He wanted, maybe even needed, to box.

Eventually, he left the hospital and moved to Phoenix, Arizona, to attend college. While there, he found a boxing gym, and eight months after his hospital release he resumed training. He shadowboxed, hit the heavy bag, and did calisthenics. But after a while, just getting in shape wasn't enough. He wanted more; that meant climbing back in the ring and sparring.

Of course, he knew the danger. He was acting against his doctor's advice and just plain common sense. So he hid his condition from his trainers. They thought he was just another quick, aggressive young amateur with good potential. At the gym, he was happy; he felt strong, just like before the accident. He fit in. To protect the fragile right side of his head, he learned to perfect his defensive skills, such as slipping punches and using footwork to dance out of danger. He also focused on keeping his hands, especially his right, high against the side of his head in good protective position. He began sparring, and even fought in amateur bouts, winning five of seven.

Although Gilmore had improved his defensive skills, punches still slipped through, whether sparring—where the action is supposed to be, but often isn't, controlled—or fighting in competitive amateur matches. Some blows hit his face and head, sometimes hard. Most of the time, the high–right hand defense worked, and he was quick enough to pick off dangerous left hooks. Sometimes though, an especially strong hook would knock the glove against the side of his head. The glove would cushion the blow, but in Jim Gilmore's condition, even a weak punch could have paralyzed or killed him. He knew all of that, but still he kept on.

Why did he take such an extreme risk? He shrugs and seems to search for an answer. "I wanted to prove I was invincible," he explains.

He wasn't invincible. After a year, he quit boxing for good. "The headaches got to be too much," he says sadly.

He was an ex-boxer at nineteen. Although his fighting career was over, his love affair with the sport wasn't. While in Arizona, he began refereeing amateur bouts, and in Washington, he hopes to become certified, if time permits, as a professional referee. He's even taken one of the necessary steps by working as an alternate referee at a recent professional match. An alternate, Gilmore explains, "just follows the ref through the prefight steps, like explaining the rules [to fighters and managers] in the dressing room before the fight."

Why become a referee? It's surely not the money. "About a hundred bucks," he says, to work four-, six-, or eight-round preliminary bouts.

That means Gilmore would have to travel. In Washington, the handful of pro fight cards are now held outside of Seattle in the smaller, blue-collar towns such as Tacoma, thirty miles to the south, or on the even more distant Indian reservations that dot the western part of the state. The boxing fans are there, not in Seattle.

For Gilmore, gas and meal costs alone would reduce his small referee's pay even more. Worse, working as a referee would take him away from his family—his wife, Michelle, and two small children—and from the grocery store that demands his attention and supports his beloved boxing gym.

Still, he's serious as well about these other phases of the sport. While becoming a referee is a goal, it's not the one he most wants. His dream, he says, is "to take a young kid, a hungry, talented kid, then train him first in the amateurs, then the pros, then who knows after that?"

On this night, no one fitting that description has walked into the gym. Seattle isn't Detroit or Philadelphia, where good fighters can be found on every block. It's not even Tacoma. But there's always tomorrow, and tomorrow he'll be training some fighters with talent and hunger. They want to fight. He tells me I should return. I say I'll try.

It's getting late, and he scans the gym floor. The young woman he'd corrected earlier is the only one left. This time she's standing in front of the mirror, shadowboxing. Her jab looks quicker, crisper, but it's still not right. She's standing too straight; the jab doesn't have enough weight behind it. It has no "pop." Slowly, he walks toward her and watches closely. He frowns, then, body coiled, he shifts his weight slightly and throws a perfect jab. It's fast and very hard. He pauses, then throws another one, then a sharp jab-cross combination. Showing is teaching. She watches and imitates. Gilmore steps back and studies her. He nods. Better. She's slightly crouched, no longer straight up. He praises her form.

Forced out of the ring by a head injury, Gilmore passes his
determination on to a younger fighter.
Photo by Peter Bacho

Maybe she's not the hungry, young kid, the future champion he'd love one day to train, but he doesn't really mind.
He's still training someone, and training's just another way
to stay in the game. And besides, there's always tomorrow.

I can't make tomorrow, but eventually, after a couple of
months, I return to the gym. Unlike the crowded scene the
first night I was there, tonight there are just a handful. A spar
is on between a tall, thin twenty-year-old welterweight
(Troy) and a stocky, thick-necked, heavier man (Mike); he's
built like a wrestler, which he once was. Mike is older and
much stronger; he outweighs the welterweight by at least
twenty pounds. Jimmy's in the corner, shouting instructions
to both fighters. The welterweight keeps moving around the
ring, always on his toes. As he moves he sticks his jab; it's fast

and long, and more often than not, it finds its mark on the fat headgear of his slower opponent. He looks slick, almost professional, and I'm surprised to learn he's just a novice.

"Keep moving," Jimmy yells to the welterweight. The welterweight's opponent takes his time and keeps moving forward. He's not discouraged by the quick jabs and hard multipunch combinations he takes from his much quicker foe. He'll take the shots because he knows that at some point, he'll be able to crowd the quicker man, maybe against the ropes, and land his more-punishing shots. The action is intense, the punches hard; both fighters are serious.

I realize that as I'm watching this spar, it's the classic matchup—the skilled boxer against the powerful puncher— the one that's thrilled boxing fans since the start of the sport (Johnson-Jeffries, Tunney-Dempsey, Ali-Frazier). I'm happy; I'm watching this drama for free.

If this had been a three-round amateur fight, Troy, the boxer, would have won easily. It isn't, at least not on that night, because Jimmy has called for a four-round spar. At the two-minute mark of the fourth round, Troy begins to tire; his legs are dead because his style of constant move-ment requires enormous energy. For a second, he's standing flat-footed in front of his opponent, moving just his upper body and head, hoping that that sort of movement alone will fake Mike out. It doesn't. The slugger steps forward— he's in range now—then launches a nicely thrown overhand left (he's left-handed) that lands squarely on Troy's chin; it drives him back toward the corner, but Troy shakes his head, bounces off the ropes, and dances—a bit slower—to midring. He was hurt, but he seems to have recovered—an important lesson for a novice. The bell rings. "That's why you stay on your toes," Jimmy says to Troy, who just nods.

"Good shot," Jimmy tells Mike as he climbs out of the ring. He has small red welts on his face, but he's smiling.

He's a slugger; this is what sluggers look like. That one punch—the overhand left—was worth the punishing wait. That's what sluggers do.

Gilmore then leaves the gym quickly, and tells Troy to lock up behind him. He has to go next door and close the store; earlier that day, the refrigerator broke. He needs to fix it. First things first. It's the store that supports Jimmy Gilmore's beloved boxing gym, not the other way around. This is Seattle, after all, not Detroit or Philadelphia.

A Guide for the New Fan

A boxing match, on either the amateur or professional level, is almost always an exciting event. The excitement is part of the sport's basic appeal: Two opponents face each other and throw punches that are designed to strike the opponent. It takes courage and skill to set foot in the ring, and that's also part of the sport's eternal attraction.

But while a viewer can see the courage, the skill is often overlooked. Watching the action in the ring and watching the action while understanding the rules and what each fighter is trying to do are as different as a fast-food hamburger and the best cut of beef. A casual viewer will only react to the most obvious action, such as a knockdown or a knockout, but will likely miss the careful steps the winning boxer took to reach that point.

In contrast to the casual watcher, a boxing fan who knows the sport will understand all of the preliminary steps — the sorts of punches and the style of fighting — that the winner employed to bring him or her to victory. In the most obvious example, a tall, thin fighter will typically use his lead hand (jab) and ring movement in boxing someone who's shorter and slower but usually stronger. In contrast, the short fighter will keep moving forward, or at least move close enough to his taller opponent to land his heavier punches. Inevitably, during such a matchup, someone will shout that the taller fighter should stop "running" and just stand still and fight. This reaction shows either the person's frustration — because

his shorter, slower fighter is losing—or his complete igno-
rance. If, for example, the tall and very quick Cassius Clay
had stood still and fought the fearsome Sonny Liston in
midring, he'd have lost, and the world would never have enjoyed the legendary champion later to be called Muhammad Ali.

In general, the world of boxing can be divided into two
halves. One is amateur, the highlight of which is the Olympic
competition every four years, and the other is professional.
Amateur rules are different from professional rules.

In amateur competition, the emphasis is on the safety of
the boxer. Thus, the gloves are usually bigger than professional gloves (generally, ten-ounce gloves versus eight- or
even six-ounce professional gloves, although eight-ounce
gloves are used in international amateur competition
among the lighter weights), and amateurs, unlike professionals, are required to wear headgear that is designed to reduce cuts and earlobe injuries. In addition, an amateur
referee, whose first priority is to protect the boxers, often
makes ample use of the "standing eight count," a practice
rare in the professional ring. This is a break in the action,
and it is designed to give the boxer, who is still standing but
has taken punches and appears to be in trouble, a chance to
recover. Amateur referees are also very quick to stop a bout
if there is any danger whatsoever to the fighter in trouble.

Moreover, amateur bouts are shorter than professional
matches. Historically, amateur contests had been three
three-minute rounds (or shorter rounds for novices and
younger boxers), as opposed to professional bouts that range
from four to twelve three-minute rounds (the latter for
championship contests). Starting in 1997, however, amateur boxing switched to the five two-minute round format.
This not only adds a minute to the total time of the bout (ten
minutes, as opposed to nine), it also increases the use of

coaching strategy during the one-minute breaks between rounds (four breaks under the new format, as opposed to two under the old).

And, indeed, strategy is what amateur boxing is all about because in this type of boxing, a good punch, properly thrown, that lands on a target area such as the face is a scoring punch. An amateur judge cannot consider the force of the blow upon an opponent, such as a knockdown. Thus, a cleanly landed jab, which is typically a lighter punch, scores a point in the same manner as a clubbing blow that knocks an opponent through the ropes. That is why some light-punching amateur boxers, who are stylish and excel under the amateur format, may not be as dominant as professionals, where heavier punches and knockdowns are counted more.

In another new addition to the amateur game, 1992 saw the use of computerized scoring at the Barcelona Olympics. Historically, scoring has been a touchy subject in international amateur competition. Charges of bias in favor of one country or against another have marred past international bouts. This electronic system was designed to reduce or eliminate the controversy. A blow that can be scored is one that lands cleanly and in the right form (the part of the glove covering the knuckles) on its target, often the head or face of the opponent. Under the electronic system, however, such a blow is counted as a score, but only if three of the five ringside judges agree. Each judge has an electronic keypad. The judges signal their agreement of a score by pressing the appropriate button on the keypad within one second of the blow.

In contrast to the "safety first" attitude of amateur boxing, where bouts can resemble an intensely physical chess match, the prize ring is a harder, more brutal arena. Unlike the world of amateur boxing, where uniform rules and safety are stressed, the regulation of prizefighting is left to individual states. This leads to a variety of rules governing the professional game. For example, while the standing eight count is not common in prizefighting, there are exceptions in states such as Washington, where the rule states that the referee can "compel a hurt contestant to take an eight count at any time."

The professional game is driven entirely by money, sometimes millions of dollars on a championship bout, and the wishes and tastes of the sporting public; that public—as revealed by its reaction to the career of former world heavyweight champion Mike Tyson—likes action in the form of knockouts, knockdowns, and hard punching. The emphasis here is on aggressive, heavy punching. This emphasis is shown not only in the change in equipment (smaller gloves and no headgear), but also in the length of the bouts (four to twelve three-minute rounds), the general absence in the professional game of the safety-driven standing eight count, and the general hesitancy of a referee to stop a bout despite injury to one or even both fighters.

In the professional ranks, fans want lots of action; most come to see knockout artists, and not clever, defense-minded fighters. If there is no knockout, the bout is determined by the judges' scorecards. Unlike their amateur counterparts, judges at professional bouts do count the force of the punch, and not just the fact that it landed cleanly in a scoring area. Thus, in the pro game, a knockdown or a blow that staggers an opponent is worth much more than a cleanly landed jab.

Under the "ten point must" system of scoring—such as the one used in California, where the professional game has a huge, avid following—the winner of a round receives ten points, the loser receives proportionately less. Normally, the winner of a round will have a one-point advantage—10 to 9—unless he/she has done something extraordinary, like knocking down or completely dominating the opponent with punishing blows. In that case, the winner will typically earn a two-point advantage—10 to 8—for that round. Fans tend to love the action of a 10–8 round.

Professional boxing, in which the purpose is to hurt the opponent, seems oddly out of place in a modern society, and possibly it is. Newspapers and books have documented well how the sport is a nasty, sometimes corrupt business. Yet, that hasn't stopped millions of fans from watching this or that favored champion, or even this or that up-and-comer, perform. And perhaps what continues to draw many fans is that among athletes, professional fighters are among the bravest, the most determined. It is that show of raw courage and supreme will in one fighter, maybe both fighters, that many fans most remember when they recall or revisit via video the greatest matches of all time, such as Muhammad Ali meeting Joe Frazier in that memorable three-bout series. Stripped of all its warts, the professional game will still produce moments of purest drama and honesty that shine in memory, that show humans, courageous and persevering, at their best. That intrigues us and will continue to do so, whether we are fight fans or not. As long as it does, prizefighting will survive, warts and all, and often despite itself.

Source Notes

Before My Time: Sammy Santos
The interview with Bobby Santos was conducted on November 11, 1997, in Seattle, Washington. For Sammy Santos versus Tod Morgan, see the *Seattle Post-Intelligencer*, October 1, 1931, p. 9.

The Ring and I: Sugar Ray Robinson versus Gene Fullmer, 1957
For Sugar Ray Robinson versus Gene Fullmer, see "18,134 Fans See Fight at Garden," *New York Times*, January 3, 1957, p. 78.

Jack Johnson versus Jim Jeffries, 1910
Tommy Burns's fight with Johnson is noted in Rex Lardner, *The Legendary Champions* (New York: American Heritage Press, 1972). For more information on Jack Johnson and the racial significance of the heavyweight title, see Jeffrey Sammons, *Beyond the Ring: The Role of Boxing in American Society* (Urbana and Chicago: University of Illinois Press, 1990). On Jack Johnson versus Jim Jeffries, see "Negro Champion Led All the Way—Jeffries Slow and Clumsy," *New York Times*, July 5, 1910, p. 2; "Sympathy with Jeffries in Defeat—Not the Fighter of Old," *New York Times*, July 5, 1910, pp. 2, 3.

Gene Tunney versus Jack Dempsey, 1926 and 1927
For records of the gate receipts at the two Dempsey-Tunney bouts, see W. C. Heinz, *The Fireside Book of Boxing* (New York: Simon and Schuster, 1961), 211, 277. For the top pay-per-view events, see "Boxing Tops Pay-per-view," *USA Today*, July 22, 1997, p. 3C. The first Dempsey-Tunney fight was recorded in "Story of the Fight by Rounds," *New York Times*, September 24, 1926, p. 1, and the second in "Fight Fast and Furious," *New York Times*, September 23, 1927, p. 1. Tex Rickard's financial loss as a result of the second Dempsey-Tunney fight was recorded in "Rickard Suffers Big Loss on Bout," *New York Times*, July 27, 1928, p. 1.

Joe Louis
For Joe Louis's reputation as a great puncher, see "The 10 Greatest Punchers of All-Time," *The Ring*, September 1997, p. 27. Joe Louis recorded the

discrepancy between his public life and private life in his autobiography, *My Life* (Hopewell, New Jersey: The Ecco Press, 1997). Louis's badly positioned left hand was noted by Jack Johnson in Nat Fleischer's anthology of boxing, *50 Years at Ringside* (New York: Fleet Publishing Corp., 1958). The Louis-Schmeling fight was recorded in "Schmeling Stops Louis in Twelfth as 45,000 Look On," *New York Times*, June 20, 1936, pp. 1, 10.

Muhammad Ali

For Cleveland Williams and the "Ali Shuffle," see "Ali's New Gimmick," *New York Times*, November 15, 1966, p. 56, and Thomas Hauser, *Muhammad Ali in Perspective* (San Francisco: Collins Publishers, 1996), 85. Jose Torres on Ali is also quoted in Hauser, p. 68. For Ali and the Vietnam War, see Sammons, p. 203; and Hauser, p. 19. For Ali versus Frazier, see "Manila—For Blood and for Money," *Sports Illustrated*, September 29, 1975, pp. 22, 24; "It Takes Two to Make a Fight," *New York Times*, October 2, 1975, p. 49; and "Lawdy, Lawdy, He's Great," *Sports Illustrated*, October 13, 1975, pp. 20, 22.

Jerry Quarry versus Joe Frazier

Jerry Quarry's response to the "white hope" tag is quoted in "The Brawler at the Threshold," *Sports Illustrated*, June 16, 1969, pp. 28, 30. Quarry's fight with Joe Frazier is recorded in "Frazier Retains Title by Defeating Quarry in Bout Halted After 7 Rounds," *New York Times*, June 24, 1969, p. 48.

A Guide for the New Fan

To refer to the safety-first attitude in amateur boxing regarding the size of gloves, see Rule 103.4(2) in the *Official Rules 1998–1999*, USA Boxing, Colorado Springs, Colorado. For amateur referee's rules, see Rules 107.6(13)(d) and (14)(b). For round formats, see the "International Amateur Boxing Association Rules," Rule VIII (A), as contained in *Official Rules*. Scoring rules can be found in the United States Olympic Committee Web site: http://www.olympic-usa.org/sports/az_3_7_3.html. For one set of rules governing the professional game, see State of Washington, *The Law Relating to Professional Athletics*, Department of Licensing: Chapter 36-12 WAC.

Suggested Further Resources

For the beginning fan, there are many easy-to-access sources that give a good introduction to both amateur and professional boxing. On the Internet, there are a number of boxing sites that give information about the amateur and professional aspects of the sport. For a good synopsis of amateur rules, general information, and history, input http://www.olympic-usa.org/sports/az_3_7_3.html, the address of the United States Olympic Committee. For a good comparison of amateur and professional rules, input http://www.boxing.ca/index.html, the Canadian Amateur Boxing Association. For those interested only in the professional game, the World Boxing Association, one of the three major governing bodies for boxing, has a Web site at http://www.wbaonline.com/.

An enthusiast looking for sources off the Internet will find that any well-stocked magazine rack has the usual staples of boxing magazines, i.e., *The Ring* and *Boxing Illustrated*. These have been joined by newer publications. All are devoted to the professional game.

If a prospective fan is interested only in amateur competition, a copy of the official amateur rules can be acquired from USA Boxing, the sport's national governing body, at One Olympic Plaza, Colorado Springs, Colorado 80909.

A public library, of course, is always a solid fallback on the history of the game; many collections feature legendary professional champions, most of them heavyweights. For example, it should be quite easy to get biographies of Muhammad Ali, Joe Louis, and Jack Johnson. These are the sorts of colorful, well-known names that can draw the public and sell books. Thus, publishers have focused on these most prominent figures in the history of the professional sport. It will be harder, however, to get biographies of obscure champions, and especially those outside of the glamorous heavyweight division.

Finally, television will occasionally show some of the historic professional bouts. Many video stores will also carry a small selection of past memorable fights. For potential fans, this is a good way to "get hooked" on the drama of the game.

Boxing History
Berger, Phil. *Blood Season: Mike Tyson and the World of Boxing.* New York: Four Walls Eight Windows, 1996.

Blewett, Bert. *The A–Z of World Boxing: An Authoritative and Entertaining Compendium of the Fight Game from Its Origins to the Present Day.* Jersey City, New Jersey: Parkwest Publishing, 1997.

Bunce, Steve, and Bob Mee. *Boxing Greats: An Illustrated History of the Legends of the Ring.* Philadelphia: Courage Books, 1998.

Knapp, Ron. *Top 10 Heavyweight Boxers.* Sports Top 10 Series. Springfield, Illinois: Enslow Publishers, Inc., 1997.

Myler, Patrick. *A Century of Boxing Greats: Inside the Ring with the Hundred Best Boxers.* Jersey City, New Jersey: Parkwest Publishing, 1998.

Roberts, James, and Alexander G. Skutt. *The Boxing Register: International Hall of Fame Official Record Book.* Ithaca, New York: McBooks, 1998.

Weston, Stanley. *The Best of the Ring: The Bible of Boxing.* Chicago: Bonus Books, 1996.

Also helpful is the Black Americans of Achievement series, whose books include:

Jakoubek, Robert E. *Jack Johnson.* Broomall, Pennsylvania: Chelsea House Publishing, 1990.

———. *Joe Louis: Heavyweight.* Broomall, Pennsylvania: Chelsea House Publishing, 1989.

Rummel, Jack. *Muhammad Ali: Heavyweight Champion.* Broomall, Pennsylvania: Chelsea House Publishing, 1988.

Boxing Anthologies

Chandler, David, et al., eds. *Boxer: An Anthology of Writing and Visual Boxing Culture.* Cambridge: MIT Press, 1996.

Heller, Peter. *In this Corner . . . ! Forty-two World Champions Tell Their Stories.* New York: Da Capo Press, 1994.

Boxing and Society

Ashe, Arthur R., et al. *A Hard Road to Glory: Boxing: The African-American in Boxing.* New York: Amistad Press, 1994.

Sammons, Jeffrey T. *Beyond the Ring: The Role of Boxing in American Society.* Sports and Society Series. Chicago: University of Illinois Press, 1990.

Boxing Fiction

Carrier, Roch. *The Boxing Champion.* Plattsburgh: Tundra Books of North New York, 1991.

Lipsyte, Robert. *The Brave.* New York: Harper Publishing, 1993.

———. *The Chief.* New York: HarperCollins, 1995.

———. *The Contender.* New York: Carousel, 1987.

Schulberg, Budd. *The Harder They Fall: A Novel.* Chicago: Ivan R. Dee Press, 1996.

Index

(Page numbers in *italic* refer to illustration.)